Springer Texts in Business and Economics

Springer Texts in Business and Economics (STBE) delivers high-quality instructional content for undergraduates and graduates in all areas of Business/Management Science and Economics. The series is comprised of self-contained books with a broad and comprehensive coverage that are suitable for class as well as for individual self-study. All texts are authored by established experts in their fields and offer a solid methodological background, often accompanied by problems and exercises.

Ulrich Bindseil • George Pantelopoulos

Introduction to Payments and Financial Market Infrastructures

Springer

Ulrich Bindseil
European Central Bank
Frankfurt am Main, Germany

George Pantelopoulos
Newcastle Business School
University of Newcastle
Newcastle, NSW, Australia

ISSN 2192-4333 ISSN 2192-4341 (electronic)
Springer Texts in Business and Economics
ISBN 978-3-031-39519-2 ISBN 978-3-031-39520-8 (eBook)
https://doi.org/10.1007/978-3-031-39520-8

This Springer imprint is published by the registered company Springer Nature Switzerland AG
The registered company address is: Gewerbestrasse 11, 6330 Cham, Switzerland

Paper in this product is recyclable.

Preface

For a long time, payments and financial market infrastructures (FMIs) have been underestimated as a topic by economists. However, almost every economic exchange and financial transaction today is matched by a payment leg, and the safety, efficiency, and immediacy of the payment, and the problem of linking the two legs of the transaction ("delivery-vs-payment"), remain universal challenges. It is not an exaggeration to say that payments are the backbone of modern open societies based on the division of labor and that any inefficiency or disruption with respect to payment and settlement has immediate and significant consequences on the real economy. Payments and FMIs are therefore also a matter of strategic importance for nation states since being excessively dependent on foreign providers has been proven to be risky as payments and FMIs can be "weaponized."

Moreover, payments and FMIs exhibit economies of scale, externalities, and sunk costs ("asset specificity"), making efficient outcomes more the exception than the rule. This raises important public policy questions, with the authorities responding in the form of regulation or acting as catalysts to direct the market into a superior equilibrium. Also, the scale and importance of payments and FMIs in the economy are considerable. It is for example estimated that retail payments alone cost around 1–2% of GDP. Last but not least, the payments and FMI space has been shaken by recent innovations, which have caused seismic shifts in payment technology, practices, and market structures. For example, mobile phones and biometric recognition have not only led to unprecedented convenience in executing retail payments but also to the entry of BigTech firms into the payment space. For the future, some believe that blockchain technology will revolutionize payments and FMIs as it would (miraculously) solve almost every challenge in this industry. Facebook's announcement of Libra/Diem, a global stablecoin based on blockchain technology, was considered by many public policymakers as a declaration of war by BigTech against the monetary sovereignty of societies.

The purpose of this book is to provide a concise but thorough introduction to payments and FMIs by offering an overview of their key functions and challenges. As a binding element, we provide wherever useful financial account representations of payments, as their examination seems to be the very basis of understanding the nature of transfer of financial claims and liabilities through the process of payment and settlement. Previous overviews of payments and financial market infrastructures can be found for example in Kokkola (2008), Banque de France (2018), and Russo (2021). These texts provide various institutional illustrations without aiming at being concise and structured theoretical texts. Berendsen (2017) falls in the latter category, while taking a very different approach than our text (notably by not relying on financial accounts as a binding element).

Beginning with an **introduction** (Chap. 1), the book outlines the various types of **risks** that are relevant to both payments and FMIs (Chap. 2) before unpacking **retail payments** (history, payment instruments and schemes) in Chap. 3 and **payment systems** (RTGS vs DNS) in Chap. 4. Given their complexity, an entire chapter is then devoted to **cross-border payments** (Chap. 5) by examining the various types of architectural arrangements of correspondent banking, as well as other cross-border payment solutions, including Fintechs, global stablecoins, and interlinked payment platforms with a competitive central FX conversion layer. The text then explores **central counterparties (CCPs)** in Chap. 6 by detailing the key activities and risk management frameworks of CCPs. Chapter 7 introduces FX operations and **Continuous Linked Settlement (CLS)** by divulging the operational mechanics of FX operations without and with CLS. This is then followed by **central securities depositories (CSDs)** in Chap. 8. The final chapter (Chap. 9) then investigates **unbacked crypto-assets, stablecoins, and central bank digital currencies**.

The book is parsimonious with respect to real-world illustrations and could of course be complemented by zooming into specific innovations, products launched, collective industry initiatives, or regulatory approaches. This allowed us to keep the text short and relatively universal and usable across jurisdictions. Earlier versions of the text have been used for some years for lectures at the TU Berlin, and we would like to thank the students for providing feedback and comments. We would also like to thank two anonymous referees for their comments, which were invaluable and improved various aspects of the text.

Without doubt, payments and FMIs will remain a quickly evolving field for which their economic and strategic importance will continue to grow. We hope that this will be mirrored by its development as a field of economics. We see this text as one contribution in that direction.

Frankfurt am Main, Germany
Newcastle, NSW, Australia

Ulrich Bindseil
George Pantelopoulos

Contents

Introduction 1

1.1 Basic Principles and Definitions

Modern economies rely on **three basic principles**: **(1) private property, (2) exchange** (i.e. the freedom of persons to change their property through consensual exchange with each other) and **(3) a medium of exchange**.

- **Property** requires a sound legal framework including how property is documented and protected. Security is important as there will always be attempts to accrue property illegally, i.e. outside the rules of voluntary contractual exchange. This also applies for property in the form of money and other financial claims (securities, derivatives, foreign currencies) and regardless of whether these are recorded electronically or not, and whether property is registered in a ledger or not. Sometimes property rights are registered in a particularly formal and protected central ledger maintained by the state (e.g. land charge register for real estate), or by private entities (central securities depositories, payment systems, bank accounts, etc.). In the latter case, property rights are often supported by legislation to enhance legal certainty. Sometimes property is assumed to be evidenced by physical ownership (e.g. in the case of cash, or in the past in the case of paper securities).
- **Exchange** includes both goods and financial assets. Goods and financial assets are mostly exchanged against money, which serves as universal means of payment. Regarding transactions in goods, only the payment leg is of interest for us here. For financial transactions, we are interested both in the payment and in the financial instrument leg (securities, foreign exchange, derivatives, etc.). The efficiency of exchange depends both on "pre-trade" and "post trade". Pre-trade infrastructures are those which facilitate communication on trade wishes (including description of the assets and prices) and the matching of trade wishes until a legally binding exchange contract is agreed. Post-trade infrastructures are those that cover all steps between the conclusion of the legally binding financial

U. Bindseil, G. Pantelopoulos, *Introduction to Payments and Financial Market Infrastructures*, Springer Texts in Business and Economics,
https://doi.org/10.1007/978-3-031-39520-8_1

exchange agreement and the settlement and legal documentation of the transfers of property. Pre-trade financial market infrastructures (stock exchanges, electronic trading venues, etc.) are not covered within this text.
- **Modern "fiduciary" money** was preceded by money in the form of minted commodities (gold and silver) and by reliance on promissory notes and bills of exchange. Modern money takes typically the form of standardized claims towards a central bank (central bank money) or towards a commercial bank (commercial bank money, with a promise of convertibility into central bank money). The claim is either recorded in the form of a position in an account (duly recognized by the legal system as a record of property rights) or in the form of a paper print (banknotes). Payments with book entry money have dominated for a long time for high-value payments, while banknotes mostly serve to facilitate low-value payments (but often also for illicit transactions) or as a store of value. Today, low-value payments are also beginning to become increasingly dominated by electronic payments in book entry money, with some countries (Sweden, UK, Netherlands, China) more advanced than others (Germany, Italy). In this text, we cover in principle all payments in electronic form, meaning all payments except through banknotes.

Financial claims (including money) are registered, exchanged and settled today electronically through arrangements commonly called **financial market infrastructures (FMIs)**. CPSS-IOSCO (2012, 7) defines an FMI as:

> a multilateral system among participating institutions, including the operator of the system, used for the purposes of clearing, settling, or recording payments, securities, derivatives, or other financial transactions. FMIs typically establish a set of common rules and procedures for all participants, a technical infrastructure, and a specialized risk-management framework appropriate to the risks they incur.

With regards to the organization and ownership of FMIs, CPSS-IOSCO (2012, 7) notes that they can be legally organized and owned in a variety of forms. For example, they can be established and owned by associations, or be organized as stock companies (with restricted or unrestricted share ownership), or they could be owned and operated by a central bank. FMIs may operate as for-profit or not-for-profit entities. In any case, FMIs tend to be subject to specific licensing and regulatory schemes, which may also restrict their business model and governance.

CPSS-IOSCO (2012, 7–9) distinguishes between five types of FMIs: **payment systems, central securities depositories (CSDs), securities settlement systems (SSSs), central counterparties (CCPs) and trade repositories (TRs)**. All except the latter will be treated in subsequent chapters. Trade repositories are essentially databases which are established in the context of the desire of the official sector to understand and be able to analyze transactions and positions in financial markets, for example for the sake of understanding financial stability risks at an early stage. Their classification as a FMI is less obvious.

In addition, there are specific arrangements in the context of **cross-border and cross-currency transactions** that may be associated with payment systems, although they go beyond. For example, CLS settles FX transactions on a PvP (payment-versus-payment) basis, whilst **correspondent banking** (which is not considered to fall under the definition of a FMI) allows for cross-border payments.

FMIs are normally associated with **wholesale payments**, as participants are typically financial institutions. In contrast, payments between private citizens and non-financial firms are recognized as **retail payments**. Both wholesale and retail payments settle through payment systems, but retail payments are in addition embedded in additional layers.

For example the ECB (2021) differentiates between payment instruments, schemes and arrangements: payment instruments are specifications for the electronic transfer of value between end-users, such as e.g. credit transfers, direct debits, cards, e-money, or digital payment tokens; payment schemes are the standardised rules and procedures for using the aforementioned payment instruments, as defined by the scheme's governance body. Payment arrangements provide functionalities supporting the use of electronic payment instruments, e.g. payment initiation services, payment integrators, wallets storing data, or tokenised payment account numbers.

When classifying FMIs and distinguishing between payments on one side and settlement on the other, it is useful to also distinguish **pure payments** from payments being part of **a two-leg financial market transaction which includes both payment and settlement** (with, as a special case, FX PvP settlement in which the two legs consist in cash, although in different currencies). **Pure payments may relate to:**

- **The payment side of a merchandise, service, or labor transaction:** i.e. a transaction involving a good that is not a financial instrument, and therefore is settled outside any financial market infrastructure (e.g. is delivered physically);
- **The granting or repayment of a credit** (implying that the other leg of the payment has either already taken place or will take place): this also includes coupon payments of bonds or interest rate payments on loans. Of course, one may want to classify credit transactions as having two legs in financial markets, i.e. being two-sided, even though cash flows are non-simultaneous. Therefore, the key concept of protection against principal risk through simultaneity of settlement of two legs (such as in the case of PvP and DvP) does not apply.
- **Payments relating to the collateralization of derivatives transactions:** when initial or variation margins change to keep secured a derivative position (both for CCP cleared and non-cleared derivatives)—i.e. if collateral needs to be added or can be withdrawn from a collateral account—this collateral is often in the form of cash ("cash" in the sense of electronic deposits to be transferred to an account that serves to collateralize a position). The payment of margin is therefore without a second matching leg in some other financial asset.

Key financial market transactions with **two simultaneous legs** in financial instruments are securities transactions (outright and repo). Transactions with two different currencies being exchanged against each other are FX transactions (e.g. USD against EUR). Finally, there are also some financial market transactions which imply only a non-payment leg, for example margining with provision of securities as collateral, or portfolio transfers: if a customer decides to transfer a portfolio from one bank to the other.

For **two-sided transactions**, the various steps after the commitment of a trade at time "T" are summarized under the term "post-trade". The post-trade period commences with the **recording** of the trade, denoting a registration of the commitment by the counterparties in relevant systems to process the transaction. In the case of a pure payment, the process starts with the recording of the payment instruction. Post-trade and payments are essentially based on machines running processes that change accounts and interact through extensive machine-readable **messages** from the counterparties to the relevant infrastructures and back. Typically, messages are precisely defined to ensure automated machine-to-machine communication.

Before settlement, **messages** coming from the two parties are **matched** and **reconciled** by the relevant FMIs: the respective messages are compared to establish without doubt the transfers to be made before implementing the transaction. This allows for the **confirmation** of the trade. Moreover, in some cases trades could be **netted** before settlement, meaning that obligations between or among participants via a netting arrangement are offset to reduce the number and value of ultimate settlement operations. The totality of these steps between the trade and the settlement are often referred to as the **clearing** of transactions. Eventually, **settlement** can take place ("t" days after the date that the trade was originally struck, i.e. at "T + t"), and all outstanding obligations are discharged (see e.g. the glossary of CPSS-IOSCO, 2012).

Another important concept related to settlement is that of **finality of a transfer, meaning that it has reached a status of being irrevocable and unconditional.** In the case of counterparty default, finality determines which party involved in a transaction can recover the full value of the payment and which party will not. For example, if a party (i.e. the payer) defaults on a series of payments for merchandise already obtained – and is subsequently liquidated with all claim holders due to receive a share "x" of their claims ($0 < x < 1$)—then all payees will receive the full value of the payment ($x = 1$), should the payment status already be classified as "final and irrevocable". On the other hand, if the payments are not yet final, these payees may only receive a proportion of their claim ($x < 1$) and have to await the outcome of the insolvency process.

1.2 FMIs Policy Issues

FMIs Raise Important Public Policy Issues CPSS-IOSCO (2012, 11) explains the relevance of public policy objectives and the need for regulation, supervision and oversight with references to (1) negative externalities (in particular of a socially sub-optimal risk management) and (2) natural monopoly issues (with implied market power and risk for market abuse). At the same time, it also highlights (3) that excessive competition could unduly lower risk standards.

One may try to group the issues which explain the public policy interests in FMIs as follows:

- **Systemic importance**: FMIs are by nature crucial for the financial system and for payments, and therefore also for the real economy. Often, they concentrate the settlement of transactions for huge segments of the economy, such as to reap synergies and economies of scale. In a world where banknotes are used for an ever-decreasing proportion retail payments, the entire economy depends on the safety and efficiency of electronic payment systems and other computer-based FMIs. The potential for large **negative externalities** in the event of a FMI failing implies that private incentives to reduce the probability of a failure (be it due to financial or operational risks) may be too weak to reach the level of security optimal for society.
- **As FMIs tend to be linked with each other, there is contagion risk in the instance that a FMI fails**. These links establish the overall network of infrastructures of financial markets, and in case of one FMI malfunctioning, the entire settlement process can fail. Indeed, many operations involve more than one FMI (e.g. two CSDs, or a CSD and a CCP, a payment system and a CSD, etc.).
- As IT systems, FMIs are **vulnerable to IT failures and cyber-attacks**. In the context of their systemic relevance and negative externalities of failures, this contributes to the public interest in a strong IT and cyber-risk management.
- FMIs are subject to **network externalities and economies of scales**, and often they are **natural monopolies**. This raises the well-known issues of pricing, governance, and regulation of such entities with market power. Moreover, it creates a constant tension between the advantages of competition (in terms of strong incentives and innovation potential) versus the merits of single dominant systems reaping maximum economies of scale. Standardization and interoperability may be a useful third approach which may combine the best of two worlds. In other cases, infrastructures are mutual companies owned by their users (i.e. typically financial institutions), so as to ensure that the interests of the users are considered (as external equity investors would tend to set prices above the social optimum).
- In view of their systemic role, FMIs **should avoid pro-cyclicality of their risk management frameworks so as to not contribute to financial instability.** Procyclicality refers to changes in risk-controls that are correlated with cyclical fluctuations in market and credit risks, which tend to exacerbate financial instability. For instance, CCPs accept securities subject to valuation haircuts. When market volatility and credit risks increase, they typically tighten their risk management frameworks, which implies that (i) valuation haircuts increase, and (ii) prompts the CCP to issue further margin calls from their participants. In the extreme, this can culminate in a sudden downward spiral of asset prices.

Therefore, it is in the public interest that FMIs limit procyclicality in their collateral arrangements, which can be achieved through collateral requirements and haircuts being calibrated conservatively by including periods of stressed market conditions, so that a minimal amount of tightening is needed during periods of market stress.
- **FMIs are adjacent to, or part of the monetary system** and are crucial for preserving market and funding liquidity. Therefore, their smooth functioning is essential for the ability of central banks to implement monetary policy. Inefficient and unpredictable payments will create large liquidity needs and hence lead to increased liquidity risks.
- As FMIs are of systemic importance for society, foreign ownership or even the technical reliance on foreign third-party providers may create strategic exposures in case of geopolitical conflicts, in which the **FMI could be "weaponized"** in the sense of a threat to disrupt its working, or through the effective discontinuation of its services. This possibility may in itself weaken the bargaining power of nations in geopolitical conflicts. It suggests that from a public policy perspective, independent domestic FMIs not relying fully on foreign third-party providers are preferable and should therefore be supported.

In sum, there are many reasons why FMIs can be subject to significant policy scrutiny FMI-specific regulation may be regarded as the ultimate output of the official sector's policy analysis of an industry and its likely market failures. Therefore, studying regulation and its motivation is one way to approach also the economic issues of this industry. Often the economic issues are described in the introductory sections of legislative texts.

1.3 The Role of Central Banks for FMIs

Central banks play an important role for FMIs for several reasons. First, **central banks act as providers of infrastructure**. This starts with the fact that the central bank grants accounts to banks and the capability to make credit transfers to each other, typically through a real-time gross settlement (RTGS) system which they provide. In this way, settlement occurs in **central bank money**. CPSS-IOSCO (2012, 67) expresses a preference for FMIs settling the cash-leg of operations in central bank money (and not in commercial bank money). Moreover, CPSS-IOSCO (2012, 62) emphasizes the general role of central banks as account and liquidity providers to FMIs:

> If an FMI has access to central bank accounts, payment services, securities services, or collateral management services, it should use these services, where practical, to enhance its management of liquidity risk. Cash balances at the central bank of issue, for example, offer the highest liquidity.

There are some forms of settlement which aim at being close to, **but are not identical to settlement in central bank money**. For example, if a (privately run) payment system has a separate account at the central bank (an "ancillary system" account), then it may require banks to transfer funds first from their RTGS accounts with the central bank to this central bank account of the payment system, and then it may mirror any payments made in the private payment system in sub-accounts it maintains within the central bank account. Central banks and users normally would not recognize this as real settlement in central bank money as the safety of the users' claims still depends on the soundness of the arrangement. What exactly can be regarded as settlement in central bank money is not only a philosophical, but also a policy and legal question that arises not only for private payment systems with an account with the central bank, but similarly for private securities settlement systems.

Central banks also need to be involved to some extent in collateral settlement, as they receive collateral from banks to protect their credit provision to banks. In some cases, central banks have gone beyond. For example, the Eurosystem has entered the field of providing DvP securities settlement services through TARGET2 Securities (see Chap. 8) and facilitates instant retail payments through the TARGET2 instant payment scheme (TIPS) (see Chap. 4).

Second, central banks act as **catalyst** to guide the industry towards solutions in the interest of society. Indeed, the FMI industry being a network industry in which inferior equilibria can easily materialize, central bank interventions through encouragement and moral suasion can help the industry to co-ordinate towards efficient solutions which serve both the industry and the society as a whole.

Third, they are active as **regulators and overseers of FMIs**. On the basis of their expertise and public policy objectives enshrined in their mandates, central banks are often active in the regulation and oversight of FMIs. That being said, other authorities outside the central bank can be the main overseer or supervisor of FMIs (see Chap. 2).

Finally, they are a **potential credit provider and lender of last resort (LOLR)** to FMIs as they are able to create—in principle without constraints—the ultimate form of settlement on the payment side, namely through central bank money in RTGS systems.

As an example, CCPs in the euro area have access to central bank facilities in the instance where they have a banking license (e.g. Eurex clearing AG and LCH Clearnet SA). FMIs who settle in central bank money are normally also allowed to deposit central bank money on their RTGS account and to request, under some conditions, emergency liquidity (without however an automatic right to obtain it) (see Chap. 6).

1.4 Payment and Settlement as Changes to Financial Accounts

A first requirement for understanding payments and post-trade operations is to consider how financial accounts change from the pre-trade to the eventual post-settlement state. Writing down the financial account implications provides discipline, as one needs to ensure that (i) assets = liabilities, and that (ii) every financial claim of one party is a financial liability of another party. Every flow of funds corresponding to the settlement of a financial transaction will have to be consistent and preserve these two properties. Two complications however arise in financial accounts representations:

- **Between trade and settlement, assets and liabilities are less clear-cut.** For example, when Peter sells a TV to Sandra, then immediately after the trade being struck at time T Peter still has the TV at home, and owes it to Sara. At the same time, Peter is also creditor to Sandra, as she owes him a payment.
- **The custody chain**: An investor holds securities via its bank-broker, who holds the securities with a CSD (or via another custodian with a CSD). In principle the securities must be segregated in the bank-broker's book such as to be bankruptcy remote (see e.g. IOSCO, 1996; AFME, 2016). Aside from the various legal and risk management issues that can be discussed in this context, it is important to specify here how to represent such holdings of assets via custodians in financial accounts. We will represent claims and liabilities relating to securities custody as if they would be real claims and liabilities, however keeping in mind that they are segregated pass-through (i.e. temporary) positions which should normally not create market or credit risk for the custodian.

As a basic example to illustrate the first problem, consider the following steps in the commitment and settlement of a purchase of a television say via e-bay (Table 1.1). The presentation of the accounts after commitment but before settlement is a matter of accounting conventions. We assume below that as long as the good is not "settled" (here in the sense of a physical transfer), it remains in the accounts of the seller. We also assume for the sake of simplicity that the two persons have the same bank. Further, we require a method to separate the various steps from the point at which the trade is struck at time T to final settlement at time T + t. This can be achieved through time-like "stamps" (**a1**, **a2**, etc.). Finally, the positions "X" stand for stocks prior to any transactions, whereby X varies across the accounts (i.e. each X in the table is nominally different – however, it could also be that an X is not included in some entries as the position is initially zero). Consider the following steps:

- The trade commitment (at time T) changes the books of the two persons, where Person 1 as the payee is the seller of the television, and Person 2 as the payer is the buyer **(a1)**. The lengthening of each person's balance sheets through the creation of a mutual set of **post-trade claims and liabilities** illustrates the additional risks and exposures between the commitment and the settlement process.
- The next step is for Person 2 to pay for the television **(a2)**. Only when the money has been received is Person 1 obliged to ship the television.
- The final step of the settlement involves the shipment of the television and its arrival at Person 2 **(a3)**.
- The balance sheets of both Person 1 and Person 2 have contracted again, denoting a reduction in exposures and risks.

Table 1.1 Payment and settlement in a financial money system – single bank

Country X – in currency X			
Person 1 (P1)			
Deposits with bank	X +a2	Temp. liability to P2	+a1 -a3
Television	-a3	Equity	X
Temp. claim on P2	+a1 -a2		
Person 2 (P2)			
Television	+a3	Temp. liability to P1	+a1 -a2
Deposits with bank	X -a2	Equity	X
Temp. claim on P1	+a1 -a3		
Bank X			
Other assets	X	Deposits P1	X +a2
Deposits with central bank	X	Deposits P2	X -a2
		Equity	X

1.5 Financial Messages

Multiple messages are transmitted between counterparties and FMIs in the settlement process With book entry systems, there is of course no real "transfer" of money or of securities. Actually, the idea of a transfer is an anachronism: nothing is really moving any longer from one account to the other. It simply disappears in one account, and appears in the other, without however travelling in between. The only thing that travels through networks are **messages,** and these are the necessary and sufficient basis for FMIs to change their books and to thereby record change of ownership. Messages provide sufficient evidence that some trade has occurred, and that the relevant parties have agreed that some transfer is the consequence of their agreement.

CPSS-IOSCO (2012, 119) highlights the importance that all FMIs **use standard communication formats and protocols**, which supports efficiency and reduces operations risks. Timely, reliable, and accurate communication is key for the efficiency of payment, clearing and settlement. Standardization is key to allow automation of interfaces by all participants, such as to achieve straight-through processing without the hazards and delays caused often by human intervention. In view of globalization, this ideally also applies to cross-border messages.

The financial industry has for a long time relied on message standards, with an agreed syntax and semantics. Examples of message standards include:

- ISO 15022, introduced around 1998, is still the dominant standard for securities cross-border settlement, reconciliation and corporate action processing.
- ISO 8583 is used for most credit and debit card transactions, and are exchanged between card issuing and acquiring banks, in addition to when ATMs are used.
- SWIFT MT messages have been the standard for messaging in correspondent banking, foreign exchange and documentary credits. Over 10,000 financial

institutions around the world use this standard to exchange millions of messages per day over the SWIFT network.
- ISO20022 is a new comprehensive message standard for all financial market operations messaging. They should also gradually replace SWIFT MT messages in the coming years.

Every message is defined through the fields that have to be filled in, and the format of what needs to be filled into each field. The concept of message standards can be further illustrated by exploring SWIFT MT messages. Amongst others, the following main SWIFT message categories can be defined: Category 1—Customer Payments and Cheques; Category 2—Financial Institution Transfers; Category 3—Treasury Markets—Foreign Exchange, Money Markets and Derivatives; Category 5—Securities Markets; Category 6—Treasury Markets—Commodities; Category 7—Documentary Credits and Guarantees/Standby Letters of Credit.
For example, category 1 consists of (amongst others) the following types of customer related payment messages: customer credit transfers; customer debit transfers; cheque payments. The messages in this category deal with payments, or information about payments, in which the ordering party or the beneficiary, or both, are not financial institutions. For instance:

- MT101: Request for Transfer: requests to debit a customer's account held at the receiver or at another institution.
- MT102: Multiple Customer Credit Transfer: conveys multiple payment instructions between financial institutions.
- MT103: Single customer Credit Transfer (see below).
- MT104: Direct Debit and Request for Debit Transfer: conveys direct debit instructions or requests for direct debits between financial institutions.

Consider in somewhat more detail as an example **SWIFT MT103.** As explained in the SWIFT manual (2021, 161):

> This message type is sent by or on behalf of the financial institution of the ordering customer, directly or through (a) correspondent(s), to the financial institution of the beneficiary customer. It is used to convey a funds transfer instruction in which the ordering customer or the beneficiary customer, or both, are non-financial institutions from the perspective of the Sender. This message may only be used for clean payment instructions. It must not be used to advise the remitting bank of a payment for a clean, for example, cheque, collection, nor to provide the cover for a transaction whose completion was advised separately, for example, via an MT 400.

The SWIFT manual provides the precise fields of the MT103 message, including whether they are mandatory or optional, the expected content of each field, and the specification of the content in terms of characters (number of characters and type, e.g. "numeric", "alphabetical, upper case only", etc.). The SWIFT manual also provides numerous examples, such as the following one regarding a very simple MT103 message. Narrative: Biodata G.m.b.H. orders UBS, Zürich, to pay euro

1958.47 to ABN Amro Bank, Amsterdam, for the account of H.F. Janssen. This is captured by the following MT103 message.

Sender:	UBSWCHZH80A
Receiver:	ABNANL2A
Validation Flag:	119:STP
Unique End-to-end Transaction Reference	121:4ea37e81-98ec-4014-b7a4-1ff4611b3fca
Message text:	
Sender's Reference:	:20:494931/DEV
Bank Operation Code	:23B:CRED
Value Date, Currency, Interbank Settled Amount	:32A:090828EUR1958,47
Currency, Instructed Amount:	:33B:EUR1958,47
Ordering Customer	:50 K:/122267890 BIODATA GMBH HOCHSTRASSE, 27 / 8022-ZURICH / SWITZERLAND
Beneficiary Customer	:59:/NL76502664959 H.F. JANSSEN LEDEBOERSTRAAT 27, AMSTERDAM
Details of Charges	:71A:SHA

A very extensive message category is Category 5 on Securities Markets Some message types are: MT502 Order to Buy or Sell: Instructs the purchase or sale of a given quantity of a specified financial instrument under specified conditions; MT503 Collateral Claim: Requests new or additional collateral, or the return or recall of collateral; MT504 Collateral Proposal: Proposes new or additional collateral; MT515 Client Confirmation of Purchase or Sale: Provides a detailed accounting of financial instruments purchased or sold by the Sender on behalf of the Receiver or its client. It may also convey the payment details of the purchase or sale. It may also be sent by, or via an ETC service provider; MT543 Deliver Against Payment: Instructs a delivery of financial instruments against payment. It may also be used to request a cancellation or pre-advise an instruction.

In any event, message standards are gradually migrating towards a new standard—**ISO 20022**. With the launch of the Single Euro Payments Area (SEPA) in 2012, European banks were the first in the world to deploy ISO 20022 for mass payment transactions. Also, TARGET2 Securities (in addition to TIPS, a SEPA compliant scheme) rely on ISO 20022. Nonetheless, individual standards remain commonplace in many markets, with SWIFT proprietary messages still established as the common standard for cross-border payments. Payment systems based on different standards of course imply a lack of interoperability and makes straight-through processing and automation much more difficult. Without standards, payment messages have to be converted at payment gateways, which often leads to the loss of relevant information as information may have to be truncated and then enriched. The global introduction of ISO 20022 will solve these issues and will introduce a rich data format as standard, boosting the efficiency of global payments. SWIFT started with the deployment of ISO 20022 messages for cross-border payments and cash reporting businesses in March 2023, with a co-existence period with old message standards planned to last three years. Eventually, ISO 20022 aims at covering all areas of financial messaging as foreign exchange trading and credit card payments. This should further support cost-efficiency, interoperability and straight-through processing across entire processing chains and instruments.

1.6 The Multi-Layer Structure of the Financial Money System

At the beginning of trade and the division of labor (and hence of economic efficiency and progress) stands the problem of the double co-incidence of wants. This can be (and has enormously been) smoothened through two instruments. First, via the usage of **coins (minted precious metals)** that become common as means of payment, otherwise known as **commodity money**. Settling in precious metal coins is ultimate settlement, as the transaction is closed without leaving any financial positions (claims or liabilities on other parties) in the books of counterparties. However, often suitable precious metals were scarce, and relying on coins is associated with some inefficiencies (risk of theft, forgery or destruction, heavy weight, inability to produce and maintain really homogenous coins and implied adverse selection, implied need to check each coin, etc.). The division of labor was therefore also supported by **reliance on credit**, i.e. the second leg of an exchange transaction is kept for later, implying a claim of one party on the other denominated in money (e.g. silver coins, i.e. combining coinage and credit) or another good.

This text is about payments and settlement in **financial money**, and not commodity money. Financial money is some sort of sophisticated and unified version of the second method. Unless regulation prevents it, in theory every economic entity can open "accounts" with other entities, denoting that financial relationships—claims and liabilities—are founded amongst counterparties. They can be denominated in money (domestic, but also foreign), or be denominated in any other good (e.g. securities, commodities, etc.). Everybody could have accounts with everybody else, leading to multiple, multi-denomination claims and liabilities—the unstructured "IOU" ("I owe you") economy.

With "n" households and "m" goods, we could imagine to have "n(n-1)m/2" financial claim/liability relationships in the economy (the "/2" results from the assumption of bilateral netting, as if A has a claim in good x on B, then B cannot also have a claim in x on A as this should be netted immediately). If one wants to capture reality in all its complexity, one would also need to associate credit relationships with points in time at which delivery (settlement) is expected: i.e. a claim on a cow for delivery on 1 December 2030, or 1 February 2031, etc. From this starting point, the organization of exchange and credit can be moved gradually to a well-structured and parsimonious setting that leads to much shorter balance sheets while preserving the ability to trade (without re-encountering the problem of the double co-incidence of wants, or of a reliance on metal coins).

- A first key technique in improving the organization of payment, credit and settlement is to **concentrate claims and liabilities on single agents**—what one may call central counterparties. For example, between n parties, there can be "n (n − 1)/2" financial relationships (claim-liability pairs) regarding a specific good, say "cows" (here we assume that the size, weight etc. of each cow is homogenous). If instead there is a central cow counterparty (CCCP), then there are only "(n − 1)" relations left. This improves efficiency and financial stability as (i) it requires for the cow-claimants to only monitor one debtor; (ii) this debtor can aim at having a high credit quality, such as to be universally accepted in the novation of claims; (iii) it allows the CCCP to specialize in the monitoring and risk control of claims in cows on debtors. The CCCP can be implemented in theory like a modern CCP that novates claims and liabilities after the undertaking of trade (assuming that cows are sufficiently standardized). However, more likely, it can be implemented as a central cow dealer, also in view of the imperfect fungibility of cows.
- A second key technique is to **rely on money as unit of account of credit and medium of settlement**. If all claims and liabilities are expressed in units of money (avoiding to the extent possible to have claims and liabilities in cows, etc.), then the maximum number of claims and liabilities in the economy shrinks from "n(n − 1)m/2" to "n(n − 1)/2".

Combining the two could in the extreme achieve a situation in which the only claims and liabilities are in central bank money, where all parties have either a monetary claim to the central bank, or have received a loan from the central bank (presumably, even those who have received a loan will hold some central bank money as means of payment).

However, this is not what we observe. Households typically have "moral" and non-quantified claims against a number of parties: family, friends, colleagues—in this field an informal IOU economy continues to apply. Moreover, we tend to have financial claims towards a number of debtors: (i) towards the central bank (e.g. in the form of banknotes), (ii) towards one or several commercial banks (in the form of sight deposits, possibly also saving deposits), (iii) towards insurances and pension funds; (iv) towards our employer, etc. More generally, there is not only one "bank", i.e. an all-encompassing "central bank" which centralizes all money and credit in the economy. Instead, we tend to hold more commercial bank money than central bank money, also since central bank money is available to all only in the form of banknotes.

It is in this sense that in **modern financial money systems** we do not observe the "n(n − 1)" IOU economy morphing into some form of "(n − 1)" structure. CPSS (2003, 1–2) provide the following rationale:

> ... the composite of central and commercial bank money is an essential feature of the monetary system and should be preserved. A multiplicity of issuers of money preserves the advantages of competition in providing innovative and efficient means of payment and, indeed, in providing financial services generally. The regulated or licensed character of these

> issuers (commercial banks) aims at promoting their solvency and liquidity in order to preserve confidence in the currency. And the use of central bank money in payment systems puts the value of banks' liabilities to the test every day by checking their convertibility into the defined unit of value. This policy position implies a rejection of the two extreme arrangements of monobanking, where the central bank acts as the sole issuer of money, and free banking, where commercial banks provide all the money required by the economy. Neither of these corner solutions has proven to be sufficiently stable or efficient to endure.

In reality, **the financial system is "layered"**. For instance, a household or corporate pays to a supplier commercial bank money (via a credit transfer), and banks settle in an interbank payment system, which is then eventually settled in central bank money (or they can even settle through a chain of correspondent banking relationships in commercial bank money—see Chap. 5).

Another form of layering is through **indirect participation to FMIs**. Three reasons for why participation to FMIs is often layered may be identified. First, because of the loss of efficiency of large firms and of large monopolies, it may be better to limit the activities of the monopoly firm to what is really the core of the monopoly, and to organize in a competitive way what can be organized competitively. Second, from the perspective of FMIs, prudent credit risk management structure may require that they are not exposed to a high number of counterparties that are neither well known nor rated. In other words, know-your-customer requirements (both economic or regulatory) suggest specialization on one type of customer. Third, indirect participation may help addressing operational requirements: specialized intermediaries may be able to help in fulfilling the connectivity, legal, operational etc. requirements of a FMI, and offer indirect connections to the FMI to their clients which are tailor-made and more convenient to these types of clients. These intermediaries may also integrate the access of clients to various infrastructures (e.g. a retail broker allows an individual to buy both securities issued and held in custody by CSD A in country A and CSD B in country B). There may also be synergies at local level: i.e. the local bank/infrastructure has local expertise on customers and their domestic legal issues, and at the same time have the knowledge to be a member of several key CSDs and CCPs.

Indirect participants of FMIs are clients of the direct participant Either they could have been direct FMI participants themselves but have chosen otherwise for economic reasons, or technical, legal, geographical or contractual constraints may have anyway excluded their direct participation. Only the direct participants have a contractual relationship with the infrastructure and have to fulfil the FMI's access conditions and operating rules, while the indirect participants have a contractual relationship with the direct participant. If an infrastructure has few direct participants, a large portion of the transactions it processes may stem from indirect participants.

In sum, **major FMIs typically have only a limited number of direct participants**, with a higher number of indirect participants relying on their services. Consider some examples:

- **CLS** had 60 settlement members in 2018, but these offer their services based on CLS for more than 11,000 entities.
- **Custodian banks and CSDs:** most financial institutions hold their securities via the major custodian banks (the largest ones being Bank of New York Mellon and JP Morgan) and not directly with CSDs. Having one account with one major custody bank allows to indirectly access all global CSDs. Interestingly, in few European countries, even individuals can open accounts with the CSDs. For example, Euroclear Finland has close to two million direct participants of which the large majority are citizens. In contrast, Euroclear, the CSD of France, the Netherlands and Belgium, allows only financial institutions to become participants (like most other CSDs).
- **The Euro RTGS system TARGET2:** At the end of 2017, 1963 accounts were open in TARGET2, enabling transactions to be settled for 1073 direct participants, 684 indirect participants and 48,443 addressable BIC holders across the globe. In addition, 79 ancillary systems were settling transactions in TARGET2 (including 25 retail payment systems, 23 securities settlement systems and 4 central counterparties).
- **EURO1**, a private large value payment system in euro, has 51 direct participants, who are also the shareholders of in EBA clearing. Step2-T has 131 direct participants for SEPA credit transfers.
- **CCPs** also have a limited number of direct clearing members. This is also a risk management measure from the CCP perspective.
- **Correspondent banking** (although strictly speaking not a FMI) is also a multi-layered payment and settlement financial architecture, in which few major and internationally operating banks offer accounts to other banks.

References

AFME. (2016). *AFME Post Trade Division: Client Asset Protection Task Force*, AFME Principles on Asset Segregation Due Diligence and Collateral Management, September 2016.

CPSS. (2003). *The role of central bank money in payment systems*. Bank of International Settlements.

CPSS-IOSCO. (2012). *Principles for financial market infrastructures*. Bank of International Settlements.

ECB. (2021). *Eurosystem oversight framework for electronic payment instruments, schemes and arrangements*. European Central Bank.

IOSCO. (1996). *Client asset protection*. Report to the technical committee, August 1996.

SWIFT. (2021). *Message reference guide. Category 1 - Customer payments and cheques for standards MT November 2021*.

Risks, Regulation and Oversight of FMIs 2

2.1 Risks in Payments and FMIs

FMIs are subject to various risks Because of their systemic nature, a failure of any FMI is also likely to pose financial instability risks (see e.g. CPSS-IOSCO, 2012, section 2; or BdF, 2018, Chap. 17). Furthermore, instability of payment and post-trade infrastructures also implies costly disruption and ex-ante and ex-post inefficiencies. As a starting point, we can ask what can go wrong in payment and settlement and thus lead to losses?

- First, **the good can be destroyed before settlement** because of exogenous factors. This is a prominent issue for physical good delivery. For example, a good can be stolen or be damaged during physical shipment. Typically, the legal system defines who bears the loss in this case. This risk is less relevant in pure financial market transactions.
- Second, **the counterparty can default**, in the sense that debtors may not hand over the due financial instrument or payment. This could be a voluntary act with regard to the committed transaction, or relating to a general default and the seizure of the assets of the counterparty by an insolvency administrator who will liquidate the assets and distribute the realized value to all creditors on a pro-rata basis.
- Third, **the FMI could be delayed in settlement, or it could default.** If settlement or payment is delayed because (for instance) of an IT problem at the FMI, this can cause liquidity issues for counterparties and imply their own failure to deliver on commitments towards third parties. In a worst-case scenario, the FMI could itself default and be liquidated by an insolvency administrator. This would be problematic not only because of a possibly incomplete recovery of the initial claim, but also because of the lasting illiquidity of the claim and the uncertainty of the eventually recovered value.

U. Bindseil, G. Pantelopoulos, *Introduction to Payments and Financial Market Infrastructures*, Springer Texts in Business and Economics,
https://doi.org/10.1007/978-3-031-39520-8_2

- Fourth, the failure of either the counterparty or the FMI could actually be caused by a **third-party failure,** such as for example another participant of the FMI, or of a "third party" or "critical" service provider, such as a network provider.
- Fifth, the **legal system** may fail to validate the expectations of the FMI or of its participants, with losses resulting from that (see below under legal risks).

A second way to approach risks applicable to FMIs is to start from the classic risk categories in the banking sphere (as done by CPSS-IOSCO, 2012)**:**

Legal risk is the risk of the unexpected application of a law or regulation resulting in a loss. For example, legal risk encompasses the risk that a counterparty faces from an unexpected application of a law that renders contracts illegal or unenforceable, or that supports an unexpected claim against the FMI or its client. Legal risk also includes the risk of loss resulting from a delay in the recovery of financial assets or a freezing of positions resulting from a legal procedure. In cross-border as well as some domestic contexts, different bodies of law can apply to a single transaction, activity, or participant. In such instances, an FMI and its participants may face losses resulting from the unexpected application of a law, or the application of a law different from that specified in a contract by a court in a relevant jurisdiction.

Credit risk is the risk that a counterparty, whether a participant or other entity, will be unable to meet fully its financial obligations when due, or at any time in the future. FMIs and their participants may face **replacement-cost** risk (often associated with pre-settlement risk) and **principal risk** (often associated with settlement risk). Replacement-cost risk in the context of settlement is the risk of loss of unrealized gains on unsettled transactions with a counterparty (e.g. the unsettled transactions of a CCP). The resulting exposure is the cost of replacing the original transaction at current market prices. Principal risk is the risk that a counterparty will lose the full value involved in a transaction (e.g. the risk that a seller of a financial asset will irrevocably deliver the asset but not receive payment). Credit risks can also arise from other sources, such as the failure of settlement banks, custodians, or linked FMIs to meet their financial obligations.

Liquidity risk is the risk that a counterparty, whether a participant or other entity, will have insufficient funds to meet its financial obligations as and when expected, although it may be able to do so in the future. Liquidity risk includes both the risk that a seller of an asset will not receive payment when due, and that the buyer of an asset will not receive delivery when due. In both cases, the entity may have to make costly extra efforts to deliver on its own commitments (by generating cash or by borrowing or re-buying an asset). Thus, both parties to a financial transaction are potentially exposed to liquidity risk on the settlement date. Liquidity problems can create systemic contagion, particularly if they create concerns about solvency. Liquidity risk can also arise from failure or untimely delivery by settlement banks, nostro agents, custodian banks, liquidity providers, and linked FMIs.

Market risk is the risk to suffer losses from adverse movements of market prices, reducing the value of assets. It can arise in the form of replacement risk (i.e. credit risk), or if the value of collateral posted (e.g. to a CCP) declines beyond the assumed confidence level. It can also arise for the investments of an FMI (see below—investment risks).

Custody risk is the risk of losses on assets held in custody in the event of a custodian's (or sub-custodian's) insolvency, negligence, fraud, poor administration, or inadequate recordkeeping.

Investment risk is the risk of loss faced by an FMI when it invests its own or its participants' resources, such as collateral.

Operational risk is the risk that deficiencies in information systems or internal processes, human errors, management failures, or disruptions from external events will result in the reduction, deterioration, or breakdown of services provided by an FMI.

Cyber risk is one source of operational risk that is of ever-growing importance. A cyber threat is normally one in which a hostile party intentionally exploits IT vulnerabilities of an FMI, resulting in a loss of confidentiality, integrity or availability. Cyber-attacks imply risks of data corruption or prevention of system access which can force the infrastructure to stop all activity and to perform its function. Cyber risk is a type of operational risk and can also result in other risk types materializing (custody risks, liquidity risks, credit risks, etc.). Cyber-attacks can be motivated by the desire of illicit enrichment (e.g. hacking an account in order to transfer money to another account that has been opened under a false name, with the money being then immediately withdrawn in the form of banknotes), or be driven by geopolitics or be launched even by a nation state in the context of a war (e.g. Iran and North Korea being often mentioned as ready to deploy cyber-attacks on key digital infrastructures of their adversaries in the case of a war).

In the case of geopolitical warfare, the financial system is simply one other strategically important system (like energy provision, the health system, etc.) which when being disrupted in costly and very harmful for the attached nation. FMIs could also be affected by multi-purpose malware that reaches and affects them without them having been specifically targeted. Cyber criminals can constantly search for weaknesses in FMIs' systems, and cybercrime teams can deploy their creativity systematically from any place at any time. The operation of FMIs is based on the use and trust of data. To operate effectively, FMIs must therefore ensure that their transaction and position data is intact. If data issues arise, the interconnectedness of FMIs, and large number of entities in their ecosystems, could spread the impact. Traditional replication processes and architectural design principles are intended to preserve data and software in the event of a physical disruption. However, in today's cyber risk environment, these processes and principles have the potential to spread unauthorized or corrupted data to backup databases, including those within data bunkers and backup data centres. The CPMI-IOSCO (2016) provides guidance on cyber resilience for FMIs (see also Kopp et al., 2017; ECB, 2018).

General business risks are the risks related to the administration and operation of an FMI as a firm, other than stemming from one of the above-mentioned specific risk types. General business risk refers to the deterioration of financial conditions and business prospects of an FMI due to declines in its revenues or growth in its expenses, resulting in losses that must be charged against capital.

Finally, **systemic risk** is the risk that the failure of one or more FMIs or participants could also cause other participants and FMIs to be unable to meet their obligations when due, with various possible "knock-on" effects. The failure of an FMI serving large parts of the financial system would have significant adverse effects on financial markets and related actors. These would arise from unwinding or reversing payments, delaying settlement, or forcing fire sale liquidation of assets or collateral. In a worst-case scenario, the financial system could suffer a general liquidity crisis with multiple failures and feedback loops.

2.2 Mitigating Risks

A Number of Risk Management Techniques Can Mitigate Risks for FMIs and for Their Users For two-leg financial transactions (i.e. most transactions which are not pure payments), linking the two legs of the transaction strictly should address principal credit risk. This strict linking is called **"DvP"** (delivery versus payment) in securities transactions and **"PvP"** (payment versus payment) in FX transactions. More rarely, there are also DvD transactions, when one security is delivered against another (e.g. when collateral is substituted). These techniques rely of course on the legal and technical soundness of the simultaneous execution of both legs of the transaction at once. A counterparty default can thereby no longer lead to a loss because one leg has already been settled (the one where the non-defaulting counterparty delivers), while the other leg is never delivered because of the default. A prominent example is the case of the Herstatt Bank, leading to the term Herstatt risk, being the risk that one counterparty defaults after having received its payment in an FX transaction, and before it has delivered on its part. Because of the seriousness of losses that can be inflicted from principal risks, it is prescribed that FMIs should eliminate or mitigate risks through DvP, DvD or PvP settlement mechanisms (CPSS-IOSCO, 2012, 76).

Short Settlement Cycle In an ideal scenario, settlement should be achieved as quickly as possible after a trade being agreed upon. Long settlement cycles imply that there is more time for bad things to happen in between. For securities settlement, the last decade has witnessed in most countries of the world a reduction of settlement times from T + 3 to T + 2, whereby previous decades had already seen a gradual reduction from even longer cycles. In the US, T + 1 is already applicable to Treasury debt, and will become the norm for the settlement of all securities (including equities) in May 2024. For FX settlement, most markets are also currently with T + 2 settlement, although some currency pairs are settled T + 1, and different platforms try to support even T + 0 settlement (although volumes remain marginal). Settlement takes time because of the need to undertake various steps between trade commitment and settlement. Even with complete automation and straight-through processing, the processes are not instantaneous because of various interactions between different systems which have their own cycles. Beyond straight-through processing, the design of the overall settlement process with all its steps is therefore crucial for achieving the shortest possible overall settlement cycle, and is a key contribution to the reduction of settlement risk.

High Solvency, Operational Stability and Resilience of FMIs Obviously, the failure of the FMI itself is a major risk for the settlement process. Therefore, high capital buffers of the FMI (to protect it against financial losses) and sound and secure FMI processes are crucial. This includes protection against third party failures or criminal activities (e.g. failure of a network provider, cyber-crime risk, etc.).

The **recovery and continued operation of FMIs** in the instance of a failure to remain solvent or liquid is crucial to avoid the worst-case scenario of an FMI simply stopping to operate. CPMI-IOSCO (2014) considers five types of recovery tools: (1) tools to allocate uncovered losses caused by participant default; (2) tools to address uncovered liquidity shortfalls; (3) tools to replenish financial resources; (4) tools for a CCP to re-establish a matched book; and (5) tools to allocate losses not related to participant default.

Quality (solvency, rating, etc.) requirements towards FMI counterparties reduce the likelihood of failures of these counterparties to meet their obligations. Even with perfectly secure FMIs and settlement in DvP/PvP etc., counterparty failure to deliver can imply losses, predominantly because of (i) liquidity problems that the counterparty default can cause for others; (ii) the time spent with understanding the issues and cleaning up the books; (iii) legal costs; and (iv) the replacement value of the contract.

The collateralization of credit exposures protects an FMI and its participants against losses in the event of a participant default. Collateral can be provided in the form or cash or in the form of securities. Regarding securities, the FMI needs to apply eligibility criteria (e.g. bonds issued with a credit rating of at least single-A) and haircuts to the value of the collateral to ensure that the liquidation value of the collateral will (with very high probability, and even in negative market conditions) not fall short of the obligation that the collateral was supposed to protect.

Use legally sound procedures and do not rely on procedures which are subject to material legal uncertainty. This is further taken up in the next section.

2.3 Legal Certainty Issues

As payment and settlement is about an efficient, uncontestable and robust change of ownership, it is not surprising that legal certainty is an overwhelming objective for market infrastructures and for their payment, clearing and/or settlement services. CPSS-IOSCO (2012, 21–22) highlights the importance of legal risks for FMIs. The legal framework applicable in the jurisdiction and the contractual arrangements entered by FMIs and its participants define the rights and obligations of the FMI, its participants, and other relevant parties, such as custodians, service providers, and indirect participants. The contingency planning and risk management of all these parties rely on assumptions about legal rights and obligations under various scenarios, including the enforceability of expected rights. All parties face unmanageable risks if the legal basis of financial operations is flawed or uncertain, which implies various inefficiencies ex ante and ex post. It is important to note that the legal framework includes both (1) various laws regulating basic legal tools like property, contracts, insolvency, competition, and liability and (2) specific financial legislation, such as the laws and regulations on the authorization and supervision of financial markets and their infrastructure and other participants. Legal uncertainty and risk may emanate from both types of legislations. Sometimes, only court cases and the resulting ruling will reveal, create, or address legal certainty issues and may trigger new legislation or contractual changes to address these.

As there are so numerous legal issues and dimensions of relevance for FMIs, and as their manifestation is different across jurisdictions, it would go too far here to review them in more detail. As one example, consider the concept of **settlement finality**. Settlement finality is a crucial concept about when key financial risks are transferred in a payment system, and when settlement is irrevocable, in particular in the case of a participant's insolvency (see e.g. CPSS-IOSCO, 2012, 23). The key question is whether the transactions of an insolvent participant to a FMI are final and revocable, or whether insolvency administrators could argue that it is void and the payment (or delivery of a security) can thus be revoked to include the related value in the insolvency mass. In Europe, the settlement finality directive (Directive 98/26/EC of the European Parliament and of the Council of 19 May 1998 on settlement finality in payment and securities settlement) requires in Article 3.1 that:

> Transfer orders and netting shall be legally enforceable and, even in the event of insolvency proceedings against a participant, shall be binding on third parties, provided that transfer orders were entered into a system before the moment of opening of such insolvency proceedings as defined in Article 6(1).

Article 5 states that:

A transfer order may not be revoked by a participant in a system, nor by a third party, from the moment defined by the rules of that system.

Settlement finality is particularly important in relation to netting systems, in which the netting needs to rely on the assumption of finality to not create unmanageable issues of disentangling claims and liabilities of a defaulted entity after netting. In short, because of its fundamental importance for the irrevocability of funds transfers and the discharge of obligations, ambiguity on settlement finality can be a major source of uncertainty for the sound operation of the financial system.

2.4 Regulation, Supervision and Oversight of FMIs

The purpose of central bank oversight of FMIs is to (1) ensure the effectiveness and security of systems (existing ones as well as the ones being developed); (2) assess these systems against applicable standards and principles; and (3) encourage relevant adjustments where necessary.

The term "oversight" appeared in the 1990s, first for payment systems, and subsequently also for securities settlement systems and CCPs. One of the first reports on such matters was published by CPSS (2005). Following the Global Financial Crisis, a comprehensive set of principles for FMIs were then developed, as divulged in CPSS-IOSCO (2012).

A distinction is traditionally made between the concepts of **oversight and supervision**. **Oversight** is generally related to central banking activity, is based on soft law (i.e. without the power of sanction but use of persuasion, or moral suasion), and is more qualitative in nature. In contrast, **supervision** is of a regulatory nature and does include the power of sanction. Oversight activities are therefore conducted in principle under the umbrella of central banks, while supervision is more a matter for prudential authorities. However, this distinction has faded somewhat in recent years with the narrowing of the gap between oversight objectives and methods and supervisory objectives and methods (see BdF, 2018, 313–314).

In many cases, **several authorities have some responsibility towards a specific FMI or type of financial market operation**. For these reasons, legislators for FMIs (e.g. CCPs and CSDs) have defined the concepts of **competent and relevant authorities** (for a list of competent and relevant authorities within the context of the EU, see e.g. ESMA, 2021, 2022a).

Competent authorities hold direct supervisory power via regulations or legislation, and typically reside in the jurisdiction in which the FMI is established. They are responsible for the infrastructure's approval and authorization (applying the relevant regulations), and for ongoing oversight. They must keep informed the various stakeholders and consult other authorities with regard to matters of interest to them.

Relevant authorities are other authorities which have an interest in the infrastructure's proper functioning, and where necessary, participate in their oversight, even though the main responsibilities reside with the competent authorities. Relevant authorities include supervisory authorities of CCP clearing or non-clearing members. Moreover, relevant authorities also include the overseers of the platforms on which instruments are traded, of the SSSs that settle and deliver traded financial instruments, and of the infrastructures with which interoperability links have been established.

As FMIs are important for several jurisdictions, this implies that **international cooperation** between authorities is beneficial. Examples of global FMIs with co-operative oversight arrangements are CLS and SWIFT.

- **CLS Bank International** is a US banking entity based in New York qualified as single-purpose bank with limited business scope, namely to settle FX transactions. It is regulated by the Federal Reserve Board with support from the Federal Reserve Bank of New York. The latter does the prudential oversight and hosts the Oversight Committee (OC) in charge of the international cooperative supervision of the CLS system. CLS is subject to a cooperative oversight agreement between the central banks whose currencies are processed by CLS, with the Federal Reserve as lead overseer. The cooperation arrangement ensures that all central banks issuing currencies settled by CLS can participate in an orderly fashion in the system's oversight so as to ensure its consistency, safety and efficiency of the operations of CLS in all currencies. The co-operative oversight and in practice the Oversight Committee established through it ensures that CLS complies with the principles applicable to payment systems and market infrastructures, and examines changes proposed by the operator to assess their potential impact on the system's rules, operating conditions, and, in particular, its risk profile.
- **SWIFT (Society for Worldwide Interbank Financial Telecommunication)** is a Belgian limited liability cooperative company that provides messaging and connectivity services to financial institutions and infrastructures (see also Chap. 1). SWIFT's messaging services are used by more than 11,000 financial institutions in more than 200 countries and can be considered the backbone of global financial communication. SWIFT's messaging services went live in 1977 to replace the use of Telex by banks when providing instructions related to cross-border transfers. SWIFT is therefore a critical provider of services for financial institutions and market infrastructures. In view of its global role, SWIFT's oversight is orchestrated under a cooperative arrangement under the lead of the National Bank of Belgium. It includes the central banks of the other G10 countries. Oversight activities are governed by a number of bodies, namely (i) a technical group, known as the SWIFT Technical Oversight Group; (ii) at a senior level via the SWIFT Cooperative Oversight Group; (iii) the Executive Group, containing only the central banks of BE, US, UK, JP and the ECB, and which represents the oversight group in high-level discussions with SWIFT; and (iv) the

SWIFT Oversight Forum, a broader group including the oversight group members plus representatives from ten other central banks, which provides a forum for discussions on SWIFT oversight policy and priorities.

2.5 Principles for Financial Market Infrastructures

The global standards for FMIs are the **principles for financial market infrastructures (PFMIs)** (CPSS-IOSCO, 2012), which foresee in total 24 principles applicable to all major FMIs across the globe. Their introduction stems from years of discussions within the CPSS and the IOSCO. In view of their importance, we briefly list the 24 principles below and provide very brief excerpts of their definitions.

Principle 1: Legal basis An FMI should have a well-founded, clear, transparent, and enforceable legal basis for each material aspect of its activities in all relevant jurisdictions.

Principle 2: Governance An FMI should have governance arrangements that are clear and transparent, promote the safety and efficiency of the FMI, and support the stability of the broader financial system, other relevant public interest considerations, and the objectives of relevant stakeholders.

Principle 3: Framework for the comprehensive management of risks An FMI should have a sound risk-management framework for comprehensively managing legal, credit, liquidity, operational, and other risks. Credit and liquidity risk management.

Principle 4: Credit risk An FMI should effectively measure, monitor, and manage its credit exposures to participants and those arising from its payment, clearing, and settlement processes. An FMI should maintain sufficient financial resources to cover its credit exposure to each participant.

Principle 5: Collateral An FMI that requires collateral to manage its or its participants' credit exposure should accept collateral with low credit, liquidity, and market risks. An FMI should also set and enforce appropriately conservative haircuts and concentration limits.

Principle 6: Margin A CCP should cover its credit exposures to its participants for all products through an effective margin system that is risk-based and regularly reviewed.

Principle 7: Liquidity risk An FMI should effectively measure, monitor, and manage its liquidity risk. An FMI should maintain sufficient liquid resources in all relevant currencies to effect same-day and, where appropriate, intraday and multiday settlement of payment obligations with a high degree of confidence under a wide range of potential stress scenarios.

Principle 8: Settlement finality An FMI should provide clear and certain final settlement, at a minimum by the end of the value date. Where necessary or preferable, an FMI should provide final settlement intraday or in real time.

Principle 9: Money settlements An FMI should conduct its money settlements in central bank money where practical and available. If central bank money is not used, an FMI should minimise and strictly control the credit and liquidity risk arising from the use of commercial bank money.

Principle 10: Physical deliveries An FMI should clearly state its obligations with respect to the delivery of physical instruments or commodities and should identify, monitor, and manage associated risks.

Principle 11: Central securities depositories A CSD should … ensure the integrity of securities issues and minimise and manage the risks associated with the safekeeping and transfer of securities. A CSD should maintain securities in an immobilised or dematerialised form for their transfer by book entry.

Principle 12: Exchange-of-value settlement systems If an FMI settles transactions that involve the settlement of two linked obligations (for example, securities or foreign exchange transactions), it should eliminate principal risk by conditioning the final settlement of one obligation upon the final settlement of the other.

Principle 13: Participant-default rules and procedures An FMI should have effective and clearly defined rules and procedures to manage a participant default. These rules and procedures should be designed to ensure that the FMI can take timely action to contain losses and liquidity pressures and continue to meet its obligations.

Principle 14: Segregation and portability A CCP should … enable the segregation and portability of positions of a participant's customers and the collateral provided to the CCP with respect to those positions.

Principle 15: General business risk An FMI should … manage its general business risk and hold sufficient liquid net assets funded by equity to cover … losses so that it can continue operations …as a going concern …. Further, liquid net assets should at all times be sufficient to ensure a recovery or orderly wind-down of critical operations and services.

Principle 16: Custody and investment risks An FMI should safeguard its own and its participants' assets and minimise the risk of loss on and delay in access to these assets. An FMI's investments should be in instruments with minimal credit, market, and liquidity risks.

Principle 17: Operational risk An FMI should identify the plausible sources of operational risk, both internal and external, and mitigate their impact through the use of appropriate systems, policies, procedures, and controls.

Principle 18: Access and participation requirements An FMI should have objective, risk-based, and publicly disclosed criteria for participation, which permit fair and open access.

Principle 19: Tiered participation arrangements An FMI should identify, monitor, and manage the material risks to the FMI arising from tiered participation arrangements.

Principle 20: Links An FMI that establishes a link with one or more FMIs should identify, monitor, and manage link-related risks.

Principle 21: Efficiency and effectiveness An FMI should be efficient and effective in meeting the requirements of its participants and the markets it serves.

Principle 22: Communication procedures and standards An FMI should use, or at a minimum accommodate, relevant internationally accepted communication procedures and standards in order to facilitate efficient payment, clearing, settlement, and recording.

Principle 23: Disclosure of rules, key procedures, and market data An FMI should have clear and comprehensive rules and procedures and should provide sufficient information to enable participants to have an accurate understanding of the risks, fees, and other material costs they incur by participating in the FMI. All relevant rules and key procedures should be publicly disclosed.

Principle 24: Disclosure of market data by trade repositories A TR should provide timely and accurate data to relevant authorities and the public in line with their respective needs.

The PFMIs also assign **five responsibilities to authorities**, which we also summarize:

Responsibility A: Regulation, supervision and oversight of financial market infrastructures Under this responsibility, infrastructures must be subject to an appropriate and effective system of regulation, supervision and oversight by a central bank, a market regulator or another competent authority. The criteria determining the infrastructures subject to controls must be publicly available. The three types of authorities are required to supervise the infrastructures, while the legislative and regulatory framework defines their respective roles.

Responsibility B: Regulatory, supervisory, and oversight powers and resources Central banks, market authorities and other competent authorities must have the necessary powers and resources to effectively exercise their responsibilities to regulate, supervise and oversee FMIs.

Responsibility C: Disclosure of policies Central banks, market authorities and other competent authorities must clearly define and disclose their policies for regulating, supervising and overseeing FMIs.

Responsibility D: Application of the principles for financial market infrastructures Central banks, market regulators and other competent authorities must adopt and systematically apply the PFMI.

Responsibility E: Cooperation with other authorities This responsibility is key in view of the cross-border nature of globalised financial market infrastructure oversight.

2.6 Implementation of the PFMIs: The Example of the EU

The implementation of the PFMIs in the EU are broken down by infrastructure type, and are reflected in **Level 1 legislation**:

- **CCPs**: on 4 July 2012, European Regulation 648/2012 on OTC derivatives, central counterparties and trade repositories came into force (European Market Infrastructure Regulation, or EMIR), transposing into European law the PFMI applicable to CCPs and trade repositories.
- **SIPS**: on 11 August 2014, European Central Bank Regulation 2014/28 on oversight requirements for systemically important payment systems (SIPS), which implements the PFMI for systemically important payment systems within the euro area, came into force (this Regulation was subsequently revised in 2017).
- **CSDs**: on 18 September 2014, European Regulation 909/2014 concerning the improvement of securities settlement in the European Union and central securities depositories became legally binding under the Central Securities Depositories Regulation (CSDR), which transposed into European law the PFMI applicable to SSSs and CSDs.
- Aside from CCPs, SIPS and CSDs, on 3 June 2013, the ECB announced that the Governing Council had adopted the PFMI for Eurosystem oversight of all types of FMIs (see also ECB 2016).

Beyond wholesale payment infrastructures, **retail payments** have been regulated extensively within the EU. Key examples include the Interchange fee regulation, the

Payment Systems Directive 2, the E-money directive, the Payment account directive and the SEPA regulation. The exact economic motivation of legislative acts is typically provided in their introductory parts.
Legislation in the EU is often complemented by delegated legal acts through **regulatory technical standards (RTS).** These are normally prepared by the European Securities Markets Authority (ESMA), and adopted by the European Commission via **Level 2 legislation**. The RTS further specify the details of some parameters in the regulations, as in many cases specifications are more technical in nature and require more analysis. For RTS, a process is foreseen to ensure that standards are suitable to reach the objectives of the regulation. Finally, **Level 3 legislation** are Q&A documents, again typically published by ESMA (for CCPs or CSDs), or by central banks (for payment systems). The three-level architecture of the regulatory process was adopted in 2001 on the basis of the Lamfalussy report (see ESMA, 2022b).

References

BdF. (2018). *Payments and market infrastructure in the digital age*. BdF Publication.

CPMI-IOSCO. (2014). *Recovery of financial market infrastructures*. Bank of International Settlements.

CPMI-IOSCO. (2016). *Guidance on cyber resilience for financial market infrastructures*. Bank of International Settlements.

CPSS. (2005). *Central bank oversight of payment and settlement systems*. Bank of International Settlements.

CPSS-IOSCO. (2012). *Principles for financial market infrastructures*. Bank of International Settlements.

ECB. (2016). *Eurosystem oversight policy framework*. Available at: https://www.ecb.europa.eu/pub/pdf/other/eurosystemoversightpolicyframework201607.en.pdf?91ca9f2f1d0fe85eced1fb2194be5660

ECB. (2018). *Cyber resilience oversight expectations for financial market infrastructures*. Frankfurt am Main.

ESMA. (2021). *List of designated competent authorities under securitisation regulation*. Available at: https://www.esma.europa.eu/document/list-designated-competent-authorities-under-securitisation-regulation

ESMA. (2022a). *Relevant authorities for Central Securities Depositories (CSDs)*. Available at: https://www.esma.europa.eu/sites/default/files/library/esma70-151-887_csdr_list_of_relevant_authorities_art_12_.pdf

ESMA. (2022b). *Lamfulssy report*. Available at: https://www.esma.europa.eu/sites/default/files/library/2015/11/lamfalussy_report.pdf

Kopp, E., Kaffenberger, L., & Wilson, C. (2017). *Cyber risk, market failures, and financial stability*. International Monetary Fund Working Paper No. 17/185.

Retail Payments

3

3.1 Payments and Means of Payments

We begin with a number of key definitions and concepts as they are commonly used in documents and glossaries (e.g. BIS, 2016). Also, lawyers and legislators typically need clear definitions and have developed and defined key concepts relating to money and means of payments, such as those discussed in Bossu et al. (2020).

(a) Payment

A payment can be defined as a payer's transfer of a monetary claim on a party acceptable to the payee, normally to discharge a liability. Monetary claims used for payments can take the form of cash, electronic tokens, or deposit balances held at a private financial institution or at a central bank. An electronic payment involves several steps, such as its initiation, recording, message transmission, settlement finality and actual settlement. Often, multiple layers are involved in an electronic payment.

(b) Means of payment and their categorization

One way to present a taxonomy of money is in the form of a Venn-diagram (see CPMI, 2018, 5). Venn-diagrams typically focus on **four key properties of money: (1) issuer** (central bank or other); **(2) form** (digital or physical); **(3) accessibility** (widely or restricted); and **(4) technology** (peer-to-peer or account-based). A somewhat different approach is shown in Table 3.1, which aims to refine the above classifications across a number of dimensions and at the same time adds further important examples. It gives up the assumption inherent in a Venn-Diagram that concepts are efficiently classified in a binary way. Consider the following main classification categories:

U. Bindseil, G. Pantelopoulos, *Introduction to Payments and Financial Market Infrastructures*, Springer Texts in Business and Economics,
https://doi.org/10.1007/978-3-031-39520-8_3

Table 3.1 Historical, current and prospective means of payments across six classification categories

	State of matter: Material (M) Paper (P) Digital (D)	Issuer: None (N) Private (P) Public (C)	Access: All (A) Constrain (C)	Recording: Bearer based (B); central; distributed; multiple ledger (CL) (DL) (ML)	Legal Basis: None (N) Legislative (L) Contract (C)	Connectivity: Offline payments (Off) online (On) presence (P)
Historical						
(h1) Cowrie shells; early gold coins	M	N	A	B	N	Off
(h2) Gold coins 1875	M	N	A	B	L	Off
(h3) Giro banking – Venice 1300	P	P	A/C	ML	C	P
(h4) Public Giro bank, (1401-1875)	P	C	A/C	CL	L	P
(h5) Fede di Credito (Naples), 1600	P	C	A/C	CL+	L	Off
(h6) Bill of exchange, 1300-1960	P	P	A/C	B/ML	C	Off
(h7) Chinese state paper money 1000	P	C	A	B	L	Off
Current						
(c1) Banknotes	P	C	A	B	L	Off
(c2) Bank deposits with CB	D	C	C	CL	L	On
(c3) Commercial bank deposits	D	P	A/C	ML	C	On
Future						
(f1) Unbacked crypto-asset ("Bitcoin")	D	N	A	DL	N	On
(f2) Stablecoin	D	P	A/C	CL/DL/B (?)	C	On (Off)
(f3) Retail CBDC	D	C	A (C)	CL/DL/B (?)	L	On (Off)
(f4) Wholesale CBDC	D	C	C	DL	L	On

- **State of matter**: as in physics where one differentiates between solid, liquid and gas as states of matter, in the space of means of payments we distinguish between material (M), Paper (P) and Digital (D).
- **Issuer:** a means of payment can have no issuer at all (N), or private (P) or public (C) issuers. We abbreviate public issuance by "C" because most of the time central banks are the issuers of these means of payments. However, starting with China in the eleventh century, governments have issued means of payments in the form of paper money.
- **Access:** access can be open to all (A) or constrained (C), whereby in many cases there is wide, but not universal access, or certain criteria need to be fulfilled which allow for a broad set of participants.
- **Recording:** the recording of the holders, i.e. the approach to establishing the ownership of units of the means of payments and the related legitimization of the payer (in terms of both the identity and in terms of being the owner of the units of payments which are transferred in the payment) can be done via the fact of bearing the instrument (B), or via the holder and holdings being recorded in a ledger or ledgers. The ledger(s) can be a unique central ledger (CL), a distributed ledger (DL)—which is one ledger held simultaneously at multiple nodes—and multiple partial ledgers (ML) like in the case of early giro banking, correspondent banking, or layered infrastructures (the latter two are not shown in the table).
- **Legal basis:** means of payment can be established solely on the basis of convention (i.e. no legal basis—"N"), or on the basis of legislation specifically establishing a means of payment, or through contractual arrangements.
- **Connectivity:** some means of payments can be used regardless of how isolated the payer and the payee are, provided the two are close to each other (Offline—"-Off"). In other cases, at least one of the two parties (payer or payee; or a legitimate representative) needs to be physically at some specific location—e.g. the issuing bank (Presence—"P"). This was typically the case for initiating transfer orders in earlier giro banking. Today, most payments are done online—i.e. requiring electronic messaging during the recording, validation and settlement between the payer, the payee, and some central computing infrastructure (Online—"-On").**(c) Recording of positions in digital means of payments and verification of legitimacy: account vs "token" and the idea of anonymity of payments**

Money is said to be based on one of two basic technologies: **tokens of stored value or accounts**. Tokens would allow for peer-to-peer payments. **Cash is token-based**, and some digital currencies are supposed to be as well, although by definition a digital token can never be as autonomous as a physical token can be. The use of the term "digital token" is sometimes sloppy, and the ECB (2020) avoids the term and refers instead to a digital "bearer" instrument (corresponding to the idea of a peer-to-peer transfer). In difference to tokens, **deposits with the central bank and most forms of commercial bank money are account-based**. A key distinction between token and account-based money is the form of verification needed when it is exchanged. Token-based payments require the payee to verify the validity of the payment object, but not his or her identity. Counterfeiting can affect both physical and electronic tokens. In contrast, systems based on account money depend on access to the account information and the verification of the identity of the account holder. Identity theft is therefore a risk for account-based money. Identification is needed to correctly link payers and payees and to ascertain their respective account histories. That token-based means of payments do not require the verification of the identity of the payer allows for anonymity in payments, which payers may appreciate for good or bad reasons.The request for token-based electronic means of payments is therefore often motivated by the perception that with the declining use of banknotes, there should be a modern (i.e. electronic) means of payment allowing for the same anonymity, based on the absence of verifying the identity of the payer. However, replicating the anonymity associated with banknotes in the electronic space is not trivial, and needs to be emulated through sophisticated cryptographic protocols. The GNU Taler as described by Chaum et al. (2021) goes into this direction. It is important to note that the GNU Taler is an online payment instrument, which also suggests that electronic payments will always leave more traces than cash payments. Bitcoin also in principle allows for anonymity, and is therefore extensively used for illegitimate transactions, but most people hold positions of bitcoins via some broker, who requires identification, which allows the authorities to trace positions and payments.

(d) Legal tender

Beyond the simple classification of means of payments according to their legal basis made in Table 3.1, various further legal concepts are relevant for payments. Bossu et al. (2020, 8) summarize the legal understanding of the concepts of "currency", "money" and "payments instrument". **"Legal tender"** is a key attribute of currency: it entitles a debtor to discharge monetary obligations by tendering currency to the creditor. It is in this sense that electronic money and commercial bank money in general does not enjoy legal tender status. Legal tender status is therefore mostly relevant for banknotes and coins, but is not a key concept for electronic payments. This raises interesting questions in the case of an introduction of central bank digital currencies (CBDC).

3.2 A Brief History of Payments

Payments have been taking place since the very beginning of economic activity (e.g. Bindseil and Pantelopoulos, 2022a). The early history of means of payments in the form of commodity money (i.e. coined precious metals) starting around 1000 B. C. is an interesting and well-researched topic on its own. While the use of a precious metal as money allows for efficiency gains in trade relative to barter, it however has still various efficiency limitations, in particular for larger scale payments, including: structural and cyclical scarcity of specie; heterogeneity and adverse selection due to imperfect coinage and usage; fragmentation of units used; weight; risk of theft and costs of storage and transport (see e.g. Kohn, 1999a; Kahn et al., 2014).

Human interaction and trade has therefore at an early stage relied extensively on credit (indeed even before the use of commodity money—see e.g. Graeber, 2012). An **IOU-based financial system** with many agents and therefore multiple claims and liabilities however lengthens the balance sheets of agents and creates additional credit and liquidity risks for all parties and the need for costly monitoring of debtors and asserting eventual payments.

One way to avoid both the costs and problems of an IOU system is to create financial liquidity through a **homogeneous multi-unit top credit quality IOU which is accepted by all as means of payment** and store of value (i.e. financial money), and which therefore plays the same role as specie in achieving settlement finality of bilateral trades, but without any of its inconveniences. By definition, if this IOU has the highest possible credit quality, then novating financial claims towards it is always an improvement (i.e. can be regarded as "settlement" of the claim). The issuer of this universal prime IOU needs credit quality, credibility to persist, and credibility to reach scale for universal acceptance.

Financial money came into being by around the twelfth century in Italy with the advent of deposit-taking banks (Usher, 1934; De Roover, 1948; Bindseil, 2019—certainly, by the fourteenth century deposit banking was highly developed in Venice). In tandem with bills of exchange and promissory notes, early deposit banking then allowed traders to complete payments to one another even if the payer and payee held deposits at different banks (De Roover, 1953). Bills of exchange remained widely used as instruments of remittance up until the middle of the twentieth century (for a systematic review of bills of exchange, see Bindseil and Pantelopoulos, 2022b).

However, one of the main issues with early deposit-taking banks was their instability, as bank runs and failures were frequent (Lattes, 1869; Kohn, 1999b). In a bid to maintain the efficiencies of trade and commerce with early deposit banking, **early public deposit banks (i.e. central banks) were established as of the fifteenth century** (the earliest being the Taula in Barcelona in 1401). Reviews of early central banking can be found in Roberds and Velde (2014, 2016) or Bindseil (2019, 2021). Early public banks began to issue notes by the seventeenth century that were also redeemable into specie. It is widely supposed that the first to do so was the Stockholms Banco in 1661 (nonetheless, state paper-based money first emerged in China around the eleventh century).

The second half of the nineteenth century witnessed the widespread emergence of the **two-layer banking system**, where private banks hold accounts with the central bank, or with clearing systems which themselves hold accounts with the central bank to settle in central bank money as needed. Electronic money transfers and digital ledgers then emerged in the second half of the twentieth century (e.g. SWIFT), which introduced **electronic interbank messaging for payment purposes**.

3.3 Retail Payment Instruments, Schemes and Arrangements

Retail payments consist of (1) instruments, (2) schemes and (3) arrangements In its payment instruments, schemes and arrangements (PISA) framework, the ECB (2021) provides the following definitions:

- **Payment instruments** consist of personalized devices, software and/or sets of procedures agreed between end-users and payment service providers when electronic payment transfers and requested and executed.
- **Payment schemes** are a set of formal and standardized rules to enable the transfer of value between end-user via electronic payment instruments which is generally managed by a governing body.
- **Payment arrangements** are sets of operational functionalities which support end-users of payment service providers when electronic payment instruments are used. Arrangements are managed by a governing body which issues the relevant terms and conditions through which payments can be executed etc. Operational functionalities include the payment initiation and execution, in addition to the storage and/or registration of personal security credentials and/or data. These will be covered in the next chapter in the context of **payment systems**.

3.3.1 Payment Instruments

Consider the following examples of **retail payment instruments:**

Payment card are usually plastic cards with electronically stored identification data, issued by financial institutions to the cardholder allowing access to funds in the customer's bank or credit accounts and to make payments by electronic transfer (and also withdraw cash at ATMs).

Credit transfers a payment order or possibly a sequence of payment orders made for the purpose of placing funds at the disposal of the beneficiary. Both the payment instructions and the funds described therein move from the bank of the payer/ originator to the bank of the beneficiary, possibly via several other banks as intermediaries and/or more than one credit transfer system.

Direct debit pre-authorised debit on the payer's bank account initiated by the payee.

Cash withdrawals via ATM Customers withdraw banknotes (currency) from some account through some machine-readable plastic cards, implying a debiting of their account.

One of the predominant issues with respect to retail payment instruments are the **costs** incurred to society (Schmiedel et al., 2012). Therefore, the efficiency of this industry is important. There is an extensive literature attempting to compare costs of retail payments across instruments (cash, debit card, credit cards) (see e.g. Junius et al., 2022; see also Wilkinson, 2011).

3.3.2 Payment Schemes

The following **retail payment schemes** may be distinguished:

Card payment schemes card schemes are payment networks linked to payment cards, such as debit or credit cards, of which a bank can become a member, allowing it to issue cards (credit cards or debit cards) to its customers. A **debit card** enables the holder to have his purchases directly charged to funds on his account at a deposit-taking institution, whereby the debit is typically settled only on the business day after the transaction (i.e. "T + 1") implying still some credit function (which is not the case for the instant payment based payment solutions described below). A **credit card** is a card indicating that the holder has been granted a line of credit. It enables the holder to make purchases and/or withdraw cash up to a prearranged ceiling; the credit granted can be settled in full by the end of a specified period or can be settled in part, with the balance taken as extended credit. Interest is charged on the amount of any extended credit and the holder is sometimes charged an annual fee.

In Europe, a number of **national card (i.e. credit or debit) schemes** still play an important role (for an overall summary of card payments in Europe, see ECB, 2019; Emerging Payments Association EU, 2021). For example, in Germany, Girocard (a debit card), encompasses "the electronic payment system", "electronic cash" and the "Deutsche Geldautomaten-System" (German ATM system). Girocard is the most common debit card in Germany, with more than 100 million cards issued, whilst in France, Cartes Bancaires is the most widely used payment method with more than 60 million cards issued (see also BdF, 2018, 62–67).

Nonetheless, arrangements differ with respect to how many parties interact to achieve the successful settlement of a retail payment. For example, American Express and Diners Club are **three-way (or three-corner) schemes** (consumer/cardholder, merchant and card scheme). In this three-way network, the card-scheme has a contractual relationship with both consumer and merchant. Meanwhile, **four-way (or four-corner) schemes** involve—beyond the card scheme provider—(1) the cardholder, (2) the financial institution of the cardholder, called the "issuer", (3) the merchant, and (4) the financial institution of the merchant, called the "acquirer" (Occhiutto, 2020). Examples of four-way schemes include Visa and Mastercard debit and credit card schemes.

The business model of all card schemes rely on a merchant fee, i.e. the merchant does not receive the full price of the merchandise, but only after deducting a certain percentage being the fee. This fee is then split amongst the scheme provider (e.g. Visa), the acquiring bank, and the issuing bank. The fee paid by the acquiring bank to the issuing bank is called an **interchange fee.**

The economics of interchange fees and their possible misuse and effects on the efficiency of payments have been analyzed in countless studies (Ausubel, 1991; Schmalensee and Evans, 2005; Verdier, 2011; Börestam and Schmiedel, 2012). In the EU, interchange fees are capped through the interchange fee regulation (EU 2015/751), which prescribes that for debit cards, these must not surpass 0.2% and for credit cards 0.30%. The EU interchange fee regulation is generally perceived to be effective, while in the US, interchange fees and overall merchant fees tend to be significantly higher leading to a continued discussion on possible market failures related to distorting reward schemes (Wang, 2023).

Electronic money schemes electronic money institution (ELMI) is a term used in EU legislation to designate credit institutions which are governed by a simplified regulatory regime because their activity is limited to the issuance of electronic money and the provision of financial and non-financial services closely related to the issuance of electronic money. One example would be PayPal. The assets of an ELMI would typically be held in the form of deposits with banks. A major ELMI like Paypal would normally also have an entity with a banking license to not have to hold large funds with a third party bank.

Instant credit transfer schemes in the euro area, **the single European payment area (SEPA)** was a major endeavor. SEPA was about making payments within the euro area truly domestic payments, without noticing differences between payments within and across countries (see e.g. ECB, 2022). SEPA was introduced for credit transfers in 2008, followed by direct debits in 2009, and was fully implemented by 2014 in the euro area. In terms of speed, any electronic payment orders are executed within one business day. Nonetheless, the quest for speed led to the introduction of the **SEPA Instant Credit Transfer (SCT Inst.) scheme**, which is operational on a 24/7/365 basis and enables the recipient to receive their funds within ten seconds. SEPA SCT Inst. went live in 2017 (European Payments Council, 2022).

There are also a growing number of initiatives to build end-user solutions on top of SEPA SCT Inst., which aim mostly at point-of-interaction or person-to-person mobile payments solutions. Examples include Europe Klarna SCT, Bizum (ES), iDeal (NL) and Swish (SE). The “European Payments Initiative” is aimed at achieving a pan-European solution. Most of these solutions are run by groups of banks.

Going outside Europe, Brazil and India for example have been highly successful in establishing instant payment based end-user payment solutions for P2P and POI payments. The **Indian solution UPI** is sponsored by the not-for-profit National Payment Corporation of India (NPCI) owned by Indian banks and Fintechs. In 2016 NPCI delivered the Unified Payments Interface (UPI), a user-friendly, real-time payment solution based on instant payments. UPI allows end-users to add a bank account into a mobile application, allowing for seamless fund transfers and merchant payments from one place. UPI has an open protocol on which other technologies can also be built, which enables unlimited network effects. Accounts of more than

350 banks can be accessed through UPI, which has now monthly volumes above 7 billion and over 100 million monthly active users in India. The ecosystem around UPI is further developing thanks to its open architecture. For example, Bharat QR is a QR standard allowing to scan payment instructions for P2P and POI payments of UPI users. Bharat Billpay is a bill payment service achieving efficiency, reliability and safety of bill payment transactions. BHIM Aadhaar Pay enables merchants to receive digital POS payments from customers relying on the authenticating customer's biometrics. NPCI has also deployed RuPay, a domestic card scheme. Last but not least, NPCI aims at global reach via collaborations with various foreign operators to allow that merchants' POS systems accept payments from Indian tourists through UPI and RuPay platforms.

Pix was launched in November 2020, an instant payment based solution developed, managed, operated and owned by the **Central Bank of Brazil (BCB)**. It has already onboarded more than 700 financial institutions and has become quickly the most relevant payment solution in Brazil today. Pix provides a mobile digital wallet and allows end-users to initiate P2P and POS payments by using an alias or by scanning QR codes. Pix also allows specific use cases like the payment of invoices and bills (request-to-pay) between companies, payments from individual to government, businesses paying employees, etc. In just 2 years of operation Pix has experienced remarkable growth. By the end of October 2022 more than 130 million consumers—or around 87% of the Brazilian adult population—and 11 million companies used Pix for making payments.

UPI and PIX illustrate the potential of instant payment based payment solutions, and the potential of technology to allow emerging economies to overtake payment technology developments in mature industrialized countries. Moreover, different governance approaches have worked in the two countries with India relying more on private banks with the central bank acting as catalyst, while in Brazil the central bank acts as scheme owner and operator.

References

Ausubel, L. M. (1991). The failure of competition in the credit card market. *The American Economic Review*, 50–81.

BdF. (2018). *Payments and market infrastructure in the digital age*. BdF Publication.

Bindseil, U. (2019). *Central Banking before 1800: A rehabilitation*. Oxford University Press.

Bindseil, U. (2021). The future of central bank money: Digital currencies?. In Daniela Russo (Ed.) *Payments and market infrastructure two decades after the start of the European Central Bank* (pp. 290–302).

Bindseil, U., & Pantelopoulos, G. (2022a). *Towards the holy grail of cross-border payments*. European Central Bank Working Paper Series No. 2693.

Bindseil, U., & Pantelopoulos, G. (2022b). *A brief history of payment netting and settlement*. IBF Paper Series 01-2022.

BIS. (2016). *Glossary*. Available at: https://www.bis.org/cpmi/publ/d00b.htm

Börestam, A., & Schmiedel, H. (2012). Interchange fees in card payments. *Journal of Payments Strategy and Systems, 6*(1), 50–66.

Bossu, W., Itatani, M., Margulis, C., Rossi, A., Weenink, H., & Yoshinaga, A. (2020). *Legal aspects of central bank digital currency: Central bank and monetary law considerations*. International Monetary Fund. IMF Working Paper WP/20/254.

Chaum, D., Grothoff, C., & Moser, T. (2021). *How to issue a central bank digital currency*. SNB Working Paper 3/2021.

CPMI. (2018). *Central bank digital currencies*. Bank of International Settlements.

De Roover, R. (1948). *Money, banking and credit in mediaeval Bruges: A study in the origins of banking*. Mediaeval Academy of America.

De Roover, R. (1953). *L'évolution de la lettre de change, XIV-XVIIIième siècles*, Paris, A. Collin.

ECB. (2019). *Card Payments in Europe – Current landscape and future prospects: a Eurosystem perspective*. European Central Bank.

ECB. (2020). *Report on digital euro*. European Central Bank.

ECB. (2021). *Eurosystem oversight framework for electronic payment instruments, schemes and arrangements*. European Central Bank.

ECB. (2022). *Single Euro Payments Area (SEPA)*. European Central Bank. https://www.ecb.europa.eu/paym/integration/retail/sepa/html/index.en.html

Emerging Payments Association EU. (2021). *Key players in the European payments landscape*. Available at: https://www.luxembourgforfinance.com/wp-content/uploads/2021/06/EPA-EU-Key-players-in-Europe-2021.pdf

European Payments Council. (2022). *SEPA Instant Credit Transfer*. https://www.europeanpaymentscouncil.eu/what-we-do/sepainstant-credit-transfer

Graeber, D. (2012). *Debt: The first 5000 years*. Penguin.

Junius, K., Devigne, L., Honkkila, J., Jonker, N., Kajdi, L., Reijerink, J., et al. (2022). *Costs of retail payments–An overview of recent national studies in Europe*. ECB Occasional Paper No. 294.

Kahn, C., Quinn, S., & Roberds, W. (2014). Central banks and payment systems: The evolving trade-off between cost and risk. In *Norges Bank conference on the uses of central banks: Lessons from history*.

Kohn, M. (1999a). *Early deposit banking. Working Paper 99–03*, Dartmouth College.

Kohn, M. (1999b). *Bills of exchange and the money market to 1600*. Working Paper 99–04, Dartmouth College.

Lattes, E. (1869). *La liberta delle banche a Venezia dal secolo*, XIII al XVII, Valentiner e Mues Libraj-Editori.

Occhiutto, K. (2020). *The cost of card payments for merchants*. RBA Bulletin, March.

Roberds, W., & Velde, F. R. (2014). *Early public banks*. Federal Reserve Bank of Atlanta Working Paper Series No. 1014–9.

Roberds, W., & Velde, F. R. (2016). The descent of central banks (1400–1815). In *Central Banks at a crossroads: What can we learn from history*, 18–61.

Schmalensee, R., & Evans, D. S. (2005). *The economics of interchange fees and their regulation: An overview*. MIT Sloan Working Paper 4548-05.

Schmiedel, H., Kostova, G. L., & Ruttenberg, W. (2012). The social and private costs of retail payment instruments: a European perspective. *ECB Occasional paper* No. 137.

Usher, A. P. (1934). The origins of banking: The primitive bank of deposit, 1200–1600. *The Economic History Review, 4*(4), 399–428.

Verdier, M. (2011). Interchange fees in payment card systems: A survey of the literature. *Journal of Economic Surveys, 25*(2), 273–297.

Wang, L. (2023). *Payment network competition*. Stanford University Working Paper. Available at: https://luluywang.github.io/PaperRepository/payment_jmp.pdf

Wilkinson, M. (2011). *Development of retail payment systems since 1949*. Thesis submitted to the Victoria University of Wellington.

4 Payment Systems

4.1 Introduction

Payment systems can be defined as a set of **instruments, procedures, and rules for the transfer of funds between or among participants.** The system includes the participants and the entity operating the arrangement. Payment systems are typically based on an agreement between or among participants and the operator of the arrangement, and the transfer of funds is effected using an agreed-upon operational infrastructure. According to the EU Settlement Finality Directive 98/26/EC of 19th May 1998, a payment system consists of a formal arrangement:

- *"[B]etween three or more participants, without counting a possible settlement agent, a possible central counterparty, a possible clearing house or a possible indirect participant, with common rules and standardised arrangements for the execution of transfer orders between the participants ...*
- *[G]overned by the law of a Member State ...*
- *[D]esignated ... as a system and notified to the Commission by the Member State whose law is applicable, after that Member State is satisfied as to the adequacy of the rules of the system."*

The funds held by the participants in payment systems are recorded in a ledger, and transfers of funds take place by debiting the account of the payer and crediting the one of the payee in this ledger. Payment systems have their origin in private deposit banking. If one private giro bank were to have a dominating role in some place and many of the payments completed through transfers amongst its depositors, then it would come close to offering a payment system according to the definition provided above. However, no private deposit bank had a totally dominating position.

The first true full payment systems were provided by early central banks (see e.g. Bindseil, 2019, 2021), such as the Taula de Canvi (1401) in Barcelona, the Casa

U. Bindseil, G. Pantelopoulos, *Introduction to Payments and Financial Market Infrastructures*, Springer Texts in Business and Economics,
https://doi.org/10.1007/978-3-031-39520-8_4

di San Giorgio in Genoa (1407), the Banco di Rialto of Venice (1587), the Bank of Amsterdam (1609) and the Bank of Hamburg (1619). All of these banks ran payment systems, which were heavily used by merchants, the government, and wealthy individuals. The procedural rules of these banks, which all have been preserved, explain in detail the protocols for fund transfers between depositors, illustrating that they were meant to serve as a giro payment system.

Payments can also be made **outside payment systems.** For example, paying through **commodity money** or banknotes does not require a payment system. Settlement of the payment occurs through the physical hand over of the coins or banknotes. Some imagine this kind of payment through the transfer of a bearer instrument to also be possible today or in the future through "digital" tokens, but this will always require some more elaborate system and framework than in the case of physical tokens. Payments can also be made in systems of ledgers which do not qualify as a payment system, such as via correspondent banking, or in closed loop solutions like Fintech payment solutions. Examples of the latter include person-to-person (P2P) payments in PayPal or in SatisPay.

4.2 Real-Time Gross Settlement vs Deferred Net Settlement Systems

4.2.1 RTGS Systems

Real-time gross settlement (RTGS) systems settle payments continuously in real-time and on a gross basis The key advantage of RTGS systems is that payments are settled with finality when they are processed during the day, which reduces exposures between banks. However, RTGS systems require banks to have sufficient liquidity to cover the gross amount of each payment. Participants need to hold such liquidity either in the form of deposits at the central bank, or via obtaining credit from the central bank against collateral. From this perspective, one can say that the sufficient availability of collateral is a key supporting factor of a well-functioning RTGS system.

RTGS systems became predominant in the 1990s (CPSS, 1997; Bech et al., 2008, 2017), and are at the very center of the payment system for several reasons. First, most FMIs settle their payments at day end (or within the day) in the RTGS system, making them crucial from a systemic perspective. Second, all relevant banks (in the case of the euro area around 1600) have a RTGS account. Third, the RTGS system holds the accounts containing central bank money (other than banknotes). These reserves of banks are the focal point of monetary policy implementation. The overnight interest rate—the starting point of the yield curve—is the price for borrowing overnight reserves, i.e. holdings of central bank money on RTGS accounts (and on other linked central liquidity accounts). For these reasons, the central bank typically runs the RTGS system.

A number of factors determine the risks of gridlocks in RTGS systems and how much liquidity is required to avoid gridlocks (see e.g. Norman, 2010): (i) total payment volumes; (ii) the concentration of payments and the size of the largest payments (vs. a high number of small payments without size outliers, i.e. payment granularity); (iii) the irregularity of timing of payments within the day (vs. a regular, well-distributed timing); (iv) strategic payment behavior of participants to save on their own liquidity needs at the expense of others, such as in the case of late payments (vs. a collaborative payment behavior). Delaying payments may allow the payer to economize on liquidity but can also lead to delays in the settlement of payments and in the worst case to gridlocks, as payments remain unsettled because each bank is waiting for another to pay first. Even without gridlock, delayed payments may imply a concentration of payments at day-end, creating additional risks. Also, delaying payments to economize on liquidity may not work collectively, as in the end everyone is worse off, as the "liquidity saving game" is akin to a prisoner's-like dilemma.

RTGS systems rely on liquidity saving mechanisms through algorithms , which allows netting to occur without any credit risk taking nor via a novation of claims (Martin and McAndrews, 2008; Atalay et al., 2010). Algorithms match bilaterally or multilaterally individual payments that are offsetting and settle them simultaneously. This significantly lowers liquidity needs without adding any of the risks that DNS systems may imply.

To demonstrate liquidity saving mechanisms, assume that three banks (A, B, C) are connected through a payment system and that Bank A has to pay 100 units to Bank B, Bank B is required to pay 100 units to Bank C, and that Bank C must pay Bank A (Fig. 4.1). Payment obligations can be shown in a "directed graph" or "digraph", whereby we adopt the convention that the party at the origin of a vector (or arrow) is the one having a claim that needs to be settled through a payment by the party at the tip of the arrow. The mathematical theory of digraphs is reviewed by e.g. Bang-Jensen and Gutin (2007). Graph theory studies structures made up of nodes ("vertices") and links ("edges") between these nodes. An undirected graph is one in which two notes are linked symmetrically, while directed graphs link the

Fig. 4.1 Three banks with a circle of claims

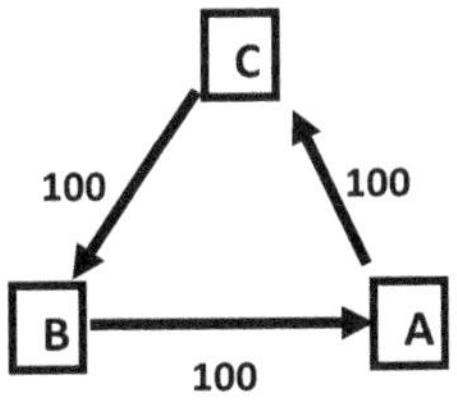

nodes in a directed, asymmetric way, which is represented by the links being shown as arrows, instead of lines.

With the help of a liquidity saving mechanism through a netting algorithm, all payments can be settled immediately (i) without any bank requiring liquidity, (ii) without any credit risks, (iii) nor with any need for novation: the circle of payment obligations can simply be cancelled out. In the absence of any liquidity-saving mechanism, the settlement of payment obligations will instead depend on the availability liquidity and the payment behavior of banks and if both are unfavorable, payments may not take place. For example, if only Bank A has liquidity of 100, the smooth functioning of all payments being settled depends on the willingness of Bank A to use its liquidity to make the payment. If Bank A initiates its payment to Bank B after the opening of the RTGS system in the morning, and if also Bank B initiates its payment soon after having received the payment from Bank A, and subsequently Bank C pays soon Bank A, then all three payments can be settled. If however Bank A is unwilling to use its liquidity as it believes that it may need the liquidity for something else, then the system may become gridlocked. Bank A may wait until late in the afternoon to be sure that it no longer needs its liquidity buffer, but that may imply that the subsequent payments of Bank B and Bank C may no longer go through before the closure of the RTGS system, and Bank A may suffer itself as it will not receive the payment of 100 from Bank C. In contrast, if all banks have liquidity of at least 100 units and do not hesitate to use it, then all payments can be processed independently and do not depend on each other, and one should assume that the payments will all take place even without liquidity saving netting algorithms.

Payment chains in practice are of course much more complex and therefore the benefits of netting algorithms and of liquidity to prevent gridlocks are much more significant. For example, the payment circle above could be one of 1000 banks instead of 3 banks. Or there could be 1000 banks with each at least 10,000 payment obligations and 10,000 expected incoming payments on that day, with these payments being of various sizes. Then the combination of the exact grid of payment obligations, liquidity buffers and netting algorithms will determine whether the RTGS payment day runs as smoothly as it should, or whether payments fail to take place on the day because of participants lacking or hoarding liquidity.

4.2.2 Deferred Net Settlement Systems

In **deferred net settlement (DNS) systems**, payment orders are cumulated throughout the day, and settlement of the net amount takes place (in the RTGS system) in central bank money at the end of the day (or possibly several times throughout the day) (CPSS, 2003). By netting payment orders, DNS systems require significantly less liquidity for settlement, and intra-day payment patterns matter far less and actually not at all in the case of a cumulation of payment orders during the entire day (Willison, 2004).

The implied disadvantage of DNS systems is that participants could be exposed to credit risks for the period during which payment orders are cumulated and settlement is deferred. Settlement finality is only achieved at the end of the day and in theory there is no certainty that the net payments will be settled as participants might lack the liquidity needed at day end to fulfil their obligations. In such a scenario, it might in the worst case be necessary that all payments have to be unwound and payments would not be settled, implying liquidity risks for all other participants. Ideally, a more efficient unwinding process allows a recalculation of obligations between the remaining participants so as to settle the highest possible number of payments. To avert these outcomes, today's **DNS systems have built-in risk mitigants**, including liquidity pay-ins, guaranteed funds, and quality criteria for participants to quasi exclude such outcomes.

Pure RTGS systems (say without any liquidity saving algorithms) and pure DNS systems (cumulating all payments until a single net settlement at day end) are theoretical extremes that are rarely found in practice. DNS systems require pre-posted liquidity and rely on several daily settlement cycles. Most RTGS systems have adopted liquidity-saving algorithms to reduce participants' liquidity needs and the likelihood of gridlocks. While one may therefore classify some of these payment systems as "hybrid", the key distinction remains that an RTGS system should not allow for any credit risks or a novation of claims related to the netting of payments.

4.3 Large Value Payment Systems vs Retail Payment Systems

Large value payment systems (LVPS) are payment systems which are used to settle larger payments between banks. These can be client payments (typically larger payments initiated by corporates), interbank payments (i.e. payments resulting from a financial transaction between banks not related to customer orders), or payments to settle claims resulting from other systems (like the day-end net positions from retail payment systems). A **retail payment system (RPS)** is a payment system in which retail payments (i.e. payments initiated by households and smaller businesses) are settled.

While normally LVPS are associated with RTGS systems and retail payments are associated with DNS systems (as the benefits of DNS increase with the granularity and number of payments, while the associated risks decrease), **this strict distinction has recently become blurred**. For example, consider Table 4.1, which provides the names of some payment systems according to the dimensions of RTGS vs DNS and LVPS vs RPS. All combinations of the two dimensions of classifications can be found. For instance in the euro area, there are two major LVPSs, one being a private hybrid system (EURO1), and one being the TARGET2 system. On the other hand, TIPS is a RPS, but settles payments on a RTGS basis in central bank money.

Consider these systems briefly one by one.

Table 4.1 RTGS vs DNS systems—LVPS vs RPS

	LVPS	RPS
RTGS	TARGET2 (ECB) CHAPS (BoE) Fedwire (US Fed)	TIPS (ECB) RT-1 (EBA Clearing—EU)[a]
DNS	EURO1 (EBA Clearing—EU) CHIPS (The Clearing House—US)	STEP2-T (EBA Clearing—EU)

[a]Normally private instant payment systems like RT-1 are not classified as RTGS systems, as real-time gross settlement does not occur in central bank money, Rather, settlement is completed in liquidity which is fully backed by central bank money

LVPS-RTGS (1): TARGET2

TARGET2 succeeded TARGET1 in 2007 and was the first integrated RTGS payment platform in the euro area. It is operated by the Eurosystem and is the largest payment system in the euro area in terms of payment volumes (see e.g. ECB, 2019). Payment orders are processed on a one-by-one, first-in, first-out basis. If a participant lacks sufficient liquidity to complete a payment, the order is placed in a queue. To reduce the probability of lacking liquidity and implied settlement delays, intra-day credit is provided on a collateralized basis and liquidity saving netting algorithms apply (ECB, 2021). According to the 2021 Target 2 annual report, 96 million payments were settled, with an average value of around EUR five million. Customer payments of banks accounted for 60% of total TARGET2 traffic in terms of volume, followed by interbank payments (27%), ancillary system payments (7.5%) and central bank operations (5.9%). At the end of 2021 a total of 78 ancillary systems were using TARGET2 for settlement purposes, including 31 retail payment systems, 22 securities settlement systems and 19 clearing houses (including four central counterparties).

LVPS-RTGS (2): CHAPS

In the UK, **the Clearing House Automated Payment System (CHAPS)** is the RTGS system run by the Bank of England, although responsibility for CHAPS was transferred to the Bank of England only in 2017. CHAPS has over 30 direct participants and over 5000 financial institutions that make CHAPS payments through direct participants (BoE, 2022). CHAPS also employs a liquidity-saving netting algorithm (Davey and Gray, 2014), with the Bank of England also providing intra-day liquidity on a collateralized basis (Becher et al., 2008).

LVPS-RTGS (3): Fedwire

In the US, **Fedwire** is the RTGS system provided by the Federal Reserve Bank of New York. As explained by the Board of Governors of the Federal Reserve System (2021), depository institutions and others hold accounts with Reserve Banks in order to effectuate payments between themselves on behalf of their customers. Fedwire is used for time critical payments (e.g. such as those between FMIs). Over 5000 institutions use the service. In 2022, a total of 196 billion transfer orders were executed with an average value of 5.4 million. The daily average value of transfer orders was therefore more than 4 trillion USD.

LVPS-DNS (1): EBA clearing's Euro1

EURO1 is a Euro LVPS developed and run by EBA Clearing, a company owned by major European banks. EURO1 went live in January 1999 with the launch of the euro. EURO1 has around 51 banks as direct participants, which are at the same time the shareholders of EBA Clearing SA. In contrast with many other operating euro area payment systems, EURO1 is pan-European, so as to provide Europe's major credit institutions a further private LVPS alongside the Eurosystem owned RTGS (TARGET2). EURO1 settles on a net basis to achieve liquidity efficiency. EURO1 achieves payment finality on a continuous basis, without waiting for participants' net positions being settled in TARGET2 at the end of the day. To contain credit risks resulting from the netting mechanism, a framework of bilateral and multilateral limits is applied. Payments are only final if they do not push a participant's bilateral position above the set limit. Each participant grants bilateral limits to each of its counterparties. These limits are composed of mandatory limit and discretionary elements. Discretionary limits can be set between EUR 0 and 50 million. In the event of a default, discretionary limits also form the basis for calculating loss allocations to the surviving participants (BdF, 2018, 120–124; see also EBA Clearing, 2022a).

LVPS-DNS (2): CHIPS

In the US, **CHIPS** is a privately run LVPS, operated by The Clearing House (a company owned by banks, similar to EBA Clearing in Europe). The Clearing House (2022) explain that the system employs a liquidity saving algorithm which matches and nets payments, either on a bilateral on multilateral basis. Although not in the strictest sense a RTGS system, CHIPS does process some payment orders on an individual basis. CHIPS has more than 40 direct participants, and processes over 400,000 payment orders per day (with an aggregate value of approximately $1.8 trillion).

RPS-RTGS (1): Target Instant Payment System (TIPS)

TIPS can be considered as an RTGS-like instant payment retail payment system run by the Eurosystem. As the ECB (2022a) explains, TIPS offers final and irrevocable settlement of instant payments in euro on a 24/7 basis on any day of the year. Payment service providers that participate in the system can hold liquidity in a dedicated account with their central bank through which payments are settled. Nonetheless, it is only possible for participants to top-up these dedicated accounts during the opening hours of TARGET2.

RPS-RTGS (2): RT1

EBA Clearing (2022b) offers a private pan-European instant payments solution called **RT1**. It is a RTGS system fully prefunded in central bank money which offers round-the-clock payment services on every day of the year. In the majority of cases, RT1 executes payments in a little over one second. On average, the system completes around 1.7 million payments per day.**Aside the pan-European systems TIPS and RT1**, the rise of instant payment systems is a global phenomenon. As CPMI (2016, 2021) explain, fast payment services for the purposes of executing retail payments on a 24/7 round-the-year basis are becoming increasingly common (see also Bech et al., 2020). The United States has more recently initiated its own system, called **FedNow**, with the private sector company The Clearing House operating a system known as **RTP** since 2018. In the UK, instant retail payments have been offered by the private sector for more than 10 years via the introduction of the **Fast Payments Service** (see e.g. Greene et al., 2018).

RPS-DNS/RTGS (1): STEP2-T

EBA Clearing also operates the **STEP2-T** retail payment system for the settlement of SEPA transactions, i.e. credit transfers or direct debits between bank customers. STEP2-T was launched in 2003 and since 2013 has been the leading retail payment system in Europe. The system actually provides different settlement services, depending on the SEPA payment instrument used. STEP2-T has around 130 members. While it initially operated in five daily settlement cycles, it migrated in 2022 to a pre-funded gross settlement approach which permits RTGS-like immediate finality. EBA Clearing (2022c) explains that under the new arrangement "[p] articipants maintain a funds balance in central bank money kept by the ECB in the technical account (TARGET2 Technical Account) for use in the system. This balance is adjusted in real time upon settlement of each individual bilateral payment instruction sent or received by the participant and funded from the participant's TARGET2 RTGS account via ASI-6-Real-Time."

4.4 Layers in Payments and Financial Accounts Illustrations

Chapter 1 had introduced the widespread phenomenon of layers in market infrastructures and payment systems. We come back to layering now in the specific context of the settlement of payments. In **retail payments** involving non-bank end-users (e.g. private citizens), **various operational layers are involved in payments**. For example, a consumer uses a front-end payment instrument at the point of interaction (POI), such as a mobile payment app linked to his or her bank account, or an overlay solution like Apple-Pay relying on a (virtual) card. Below that comes a scheme layer, such as in Europe SEPA SCT INST (for instant payments) or a card scheme. Next comes a clearing layer, and eventually, a settlement layer. The case of retail payment solutions based on instant payments is particularly open to various modules at the different levels, while e.g. credit-card or e-money scheme-based payments tend to be more integrated and proprietary. PayPal with settlement in commercial bank money through a direct debit is another example on how solutions can be combined across the layers. However, this layering was not necessarily equivalent to the layering of actual settlements.

Table 4.2 Payment with single bank

Country X – in currency X			
Person 1			
Other assets	X	Equity	X
Car	+a		
Deposits at bank	X -a		
Person 2			
Other assets	X	Equity	X
Car	-a		
Deposits at bank	X +a		
Bank			
Other assets	X	Deposits Person 1	X -a
Deposits at central bank	X	Deposits Person 2	X +a
		Equity	X

In what follows, we focus on the settlement process and distinguish between payments with a **single settlement layer**, and those which involve **two settlement layers** and illustrate various such cases in financial accounts. Also, an example with **three settlement layers** will be presented.

4.4.1 Single Settlement Layer Payments

1. **All traders have accounts in one bank**
   Consider a first example of a single layer payment system in which everyone has accounts with one commercial bank, where Person 2 sells a car to Person 1 via a transfer of bank deposits (Table 4.2).

A similar structure is obtained if instead of the bank offering deposit accounts, a closed loop Fintech provider like PayPal or SatisPay provides a person-to-person payment solution (see e.g. Chap. 5).

2. **Correspondent banking**
   In correspondent banking, banks debit or credit mutual accounts (vostro/nostro/loro accounts) instead of settling a transfer through a payment system. It is still common in cross-border payments and will be presented in that context in Chap. 5. Below we once again assume that Person 2 sells a car to Person 1 (Table 4.3).

Table 4.3 Payment with correspondent banking

Country X – in currency X			
Person 1			
Other assets	X	Equity	X
Car	+a		
Deposits at Bank 1	X -a		
Bank 1			
Nostro with Bank 2	X -a	Deposits Person 1	X -a
Other assets	X	Vostro Bank 2	X
Deposits at central bank	X	Equity	X
Bank 2			
Nostro with Bank 1	X	Deposits Person 2	X +a
Other assets	X	Vostro Bank 1	X -a
Deposits at central bank	X	Equity	X
Person 2			
Other assets	X	Equity	X
Car	-a		
Deposits at Bank 2	X +a		

Table 4.4 Interbank payment

Country X – in currency X			
Bank 1			
Other assets	X	Deposits	X
Deposits at central bank	X +a	Credit from Bank 2	+a
		Equity	X
Bank 2			
Other assets	X	Deposits	X
Deposits at central bank	X -a	Equity	X
Credit to Bank 1	+a		
Central Bank X			
Other assets	X	Deposits Bank 1	X +a
		Deposits Bank 2	X -a
		Banknotes	X
		Equity	X

3. **Pure interbank-payments**
   Another form of a single settlement layer payment occurs when banks who have access to the central bank grant to each other interbank loans (i.e. pure interbank transactions). Below we assume that Bank 2 grants an interbank loan to Bank 1 (repaid sometime in the future, which is not shown below), which is settled in the RTGS system with the central bank (Table 4.4).

4. **Direct payments in central bank money**
   A final example of a single settlement layer payment is one where Person 1 purchases a car from Person 2 by paying directly either with (i) banknotes or (ii) CBDC (Table 4.5).

Table 4.5 Payment with banknotes

Country X – in currency X			
Person 1			
Other assets	X	Equity	X
Car	+a		
Banknotes	X -a		
Person 2			
Other assets	X	Equity	X
Car	-a		
Banknotes	X +a		
Central Bank			
Other assets	X	Banknotes	X
		Equity	X

Table 4.6 Payment with account-based CBDC

Country X – in currency X			
Person 1			
Other assets	X	Equity	X
Car	+a		
CBDC	X -a		
Person 2			
Other assets	X	Equity	X
Car	-a		
CBDC	X +a		
Central Bank			
Other assets	X	CBDC Person 1	X -a
		CBDC Person 2	X +a
		Banknotes	X
		Equity	X

Although payment in a "token-based" anonymous form of CBDC would not register on the books of the central bank (i.e. analogous to payments in banknotes), an account-based form of CBDC (see Chap. 9) would give rise to changes in the ledger of the central bank (Table 4.6).

4.4.2 Double Settlement Layer Payments

1. **Withdrawal of banknotes by Person 1 to purchase a car, payment with banknotes to Person 2, return of banknote by Person 2 to their bank**
   An indirect involvement of a second payment layer occurs in this case. Banknotes are used for the payment, but eventually Person 2 re-adjusts their banknote holdings by returning them to their bank. Hence, banknotes are used only

Table 4.7 Payment with banknotes, banknotes then returned to the central bank

Country X – in currency X			
Person 1			
Other assets	X	Equity	X
Car	+a2		
Deposits at Bank 1	X **-a1**		
Banknotes	X **+a1** -a2		
Bank 1			
Other assets	X	Deposits Person 1	X **-a1**
Deposits at central bank	X **-a1**	Equity	X
Bank 2			
Other assets	X	Deposits Person 2	X +a3
Deposits at central bank	X +a3	Equity	X
Person 2			
Other assets	X	Equity	X
Car	-a2		
Deposits at Bank 2	X +a3		
Banknotes	X +a2 -a3		
Central Bank X			
Other assets	X	Deposits Bank 1	X **-a1**
		Deposits Bank 2	X +a3
		Banknotes	X **+a1** -a3
		Equity	X

temporarily for settlement, but ultimate settlement is in commercial bank money. This may be the case because there is a hesitance to hold large amounts of banknotes for custody risk reasons, as it is feared that the banknotes could be destroyed or stolen. Consider the following steps:

- Person 1 withdraws some banknotes from an ATM of Bank 1 **(a1)**.
- Person 1 then purchases the car with banknotes from Person 2 **(a2)**.
- Person 2 returns the banknotes into their bank, which passes them on immediately to the central bank **(a3)** (Table 4.7).

2. **Retail payment system with instant settlement via ACH: no prefunding**
   Now we illustrate the typical two settlement layer retail payment through credit transfers, assuming that the different steps are not simultaneous. The retail payment system is captured in the accounts of a private **automated clearing house (ACH)**. Although it is assumed in the case below that the banks can have negative balances during the day on their accounts with the ACH, any negative positions need to be rectified by the end of the day.
   - In this case, Person 2 sells a car to Person 1, and here Person 1 makes a payment from their bank account (e.g. via a mobile phone banking app) to the bank account of Person 2. The bank account of Person 1 is debited immediately **(a1).** We assume that Person 2 could verify this and hands over the car at the same moment.

- Bank 1 then submits the transaction to the ACH and the ACH transfer the funds from Bank 1 to Bank 2 within the ACH's ledger, i.e. the position of the two banks towards the ACH are now respectively credited or debited **(a2)**.
- The end of day settlement period now begins, with the transaction settled in the RTGS system, and the ACH deposits of each bank are zeroed **(a3)**. In the absence of other client transfer orders in our hypothetical example, the squaring of the accounts covers exactly the impact of the one transfer order processed.
- Bank 2 receives the payment message in the context of the ACH fund transfer that provides it with the necessary information on the nature of the transfer and the associated need to credit a bank account of one of its depositors—i.e. Person 2 **(a4)**. This crediting could occur the next day, or also on the same day before the end of day closing of the ACH.

Note that due to the sequential timing of the flows (with four subsequent events in the financial accounts), IOUs are created at several stages (and disappear again when settlement occurs). These are typical to non-simultaneous multiple layer payment processes and imply the temporary lengthening of balance sheets. We do not show these IOUs in the accounts below for the sake of simplicity. For example, Bank 1 debits the deposit account of Person 1 at the point of time 1 (a1), but the debit of the Bank 1's account with the ACH only occurs somewhat later, at point of time 2 (a2). In between, Bank 1 must have an IOU like liability to Person 1, which is discharged once its ACH account is debited. At that time the IOU claim of Person 1 towards Bank 1 becomes an IOU claim of Person 1 on the ACH. Moreover, between points in time 1 and 4, Person 1 has an IOU type liability to Person 2 as the latter has handed over the car but not received a payment. In case of a default in the financial system between points in time 1 and 4, the question of who is liable to losses (i.e. who is really the obligor of these temporary IOUs) would be tested probably in court. This illustrates the importance of legal certainty and settlement finality. Also note that in the complete absence of pre-funding the ACH, there is not even an ancillary system account needed for the ACH in the RTGS system – only net settlement instructions between banks need to be transmitted from the ACH to the RTGS system (Table 4.8).

The fact that the ACH accepts negative balances on bank deposit accounts would imply credit exposures of the ACH (and of the banks running positive balances), which are normally not accepted. To reduce this credit risk, it could for example be required that negative balances are collateralized.

Table 4.8 Payment with bank transfer via ACH

Country X – in currency X					
Person 1					
Other assets	X		Equity	X	
Car	**+a1**				
Deposits at Bank 1	X **-a1**				
Banknotes	X				
Bank 1					
Other assets	X		Deposits Person 1	X **-a1**	
Deposits at central bank	X	-a3	Equity	X	
Deposits at ACH		-a2 +a3			
ACH					
Other assets	X		Deposits Bank 1		-a2 +a3
			Deposits Bank 2		+a2 -a3
			Other Liabilities	X	
Bank 2					
Other assets	X		Deposits Person 2	X	+a4
Deposits at central bank	X	+a3	Equity	X	
Deposits at ACH		+a2 -a3			
Person 2					
Other assets	X		Equity	X	
Car	**-a1**				
Deposits at Bank 2	X	+a4			
Banknotes	X				
Central Bank X					
Other assets	X		Deposits Bank 1	X	-a3
			Deposits Bank 2	X	+a3
			Banknotes	X	
			Equity	X	

3. **Retail instant payments: when the ACH is fully pre-funded**
   In the euro area, private payment systems offering instant payments rely on a **fully prefunding mechanism** in central bank money. It might be argued that prefunding mechanisms allow the ACH to offer settlement in central bank money, but that is not true. Rather, **settlement is backed by central bank money** while the ACH offers settlement finality on its own books. In most countries, the construct is such that banks have a claim on the ACH funds held at the central bank in case the ACH defaults.

   Fully prefunded ACHs can operate **with or without a daily defunding operation in which the ACH accounts are brought back to zero**. In what follows, we assume that accounts within the ACH must be brought back to zero through an end-of-day defunding operation, and that Person 1 purchases a car from Person 2 through an instant payment. If a daily funding and de-funding cycle is foreseen, then in the morning the funding transfers take place all before the ACH operations begin. However, in a 24/7 system, funding (and de-funding) occurs any time during operating hours of the RTGS system and some liquidity is always kept by banks on their ACH account because payments must remain possible. Consider the following steps:

Table 4.9 Payment with instant payment via ACH with prefunded central bank money

Eurosystem – in euros			
Person 1			
Other assets	X	Equity	X
Car	+c		
Deposits at Bank 1	X -c		
Banknotes	X		
Bank 1			
Other assets	X	Deposits Person 1	X -c
Deposits at central bank	X -a +d	Equity	X
Deposits at ACH	+a -c -d		
ACH			
Other assets	X	Deposits Bank 1	X +a -c -d
Deposits at central bank	+a +b -d -e	Deposits Bank 2	X +b +c -e
		Other Liabilities	X
Bank 2			
Other assets	X	Deposits Person 2	X +c
Deposits at central bank	X -b +e	Equity	X
Deposits at ACH	+b +c -e		
Person 2			
Other assets	X	Equity	X
Car	-c		
Deposits at Bank 2	X +c		
Banknotes	X		
Central Bank			
Other assets	X	Deposits Bank 1	X -a +d
		Deposits Bank 2	X -b +e
		Banknotes	X
		Deposits ACH	X +a +b -d -e
		Equity	X

- The banks pre-fund the ACH, whereby Bank 1 transfers in an amount of "a" and Bank 2 an amount of "b" (these amounts could also be negative, if the bank perceives its ACH account to be over-liquid). This can occur at any time during RTGS operating hours. The size of the pay-ins depend on the outflows experienced previously and the expectations of further flows until the next planned funding or defunding operation.
- Person 1 then purchases the car from Person 2 with a value of "c", paying via an instant payment banking app, and the payment being immediately settled in the books of the ACH where the account of Bank 1 is debited and the account of Bank 2 credited.
- There is no end-of-day defunding cycle, but banks may want to adjust their position with the ACH before the RTGS system closes. The transfer from the ACH to Bank 1 in the RTGS system is "d" and from the ACH to Bank 2 is "e". Note that a, b, d, and e could in principle be negative, provided the net position of the bank in the ACH stays always positive (Table 4.9).

As there is no daily de-funding cycle, the ACH can operate 24 h per day. Banks however need to replenish (or deplete) their ACH deposit account during the operating hours of the RTGS system and have to anticipate the possible outflows from the ACH account during the closing hours of the RTGS system. On the other hand, defunding operations can be made any time during RTGS operating hours if a respective bank were to feel that it has accumulated unnecessarily large balances on the books of the ACH (e.g. Bank 2 in this case).

4.4.3 Triple Settlement Layer Payments

Case of Several ACHs/Payment Systems Co-existing

The finality that an ACH provides for instant payments as described in the above example raises the question of how instant payments can be settled if the **banks of the payer and payee are connected to different ACHs**. This is rectified through **interoperability**, in which two ACHs use a common "hub", and subsequently move their **RTGS cash accounts from the central bank to the hub**. In this way, the hub provides the link between the ACHs. An example of such an arrangement in the euro area is TIPS, where 11 ACHs recently shifted their cash accounts from TARGET2 to TIPS for the purposes of settling instant payments (see ECB, 2022b).

Consider the following case:

- Bank 1 relies on ACH 1 and Bank 2 relies on ACH 2.
- The two ACHs are connected and hold funds at a common hub (e.g. TIPS).
- As a starting point, each bank loads onto their account with their respective ACH, and each ACH holds the funds within its account in TIPS **(a, b)**.
- Upon Person 1 purchasing a car from Person 2 in the amount of "c", the instant payment is settled through TIPS **(c)** (Table 4.10).

Table 4.10 Payment with instant payment via ACH with prefunded central bank money

Eurosystem – in euros			
Person 1			
Other assets	X	Equity	X
Car	+c		
Deposits at Bank 1	X -c		
Banknotes	X		
Bank 1			
Other assets	X	Deposits Person 1	X -c
Deposits at central bank	X -a	Equity	X
Deposits at ACH 1	+a -c		
ACH 1			
TIPS account	+a -c	Deposits Bank 1	+a -c
Other assets	X	Other Liabilities	X
TIPS			
Deposits at central bank	+a +b	ACH 1	+a -c
		ACH 2	+b +c
ACH 2			
TIPS account	+b +c	Deposits Bank 2	+b +c
Other assets		Other Liabilities	X
Bank 2			
Other assets	X	Deposits Person 2	X +c
Deposits at central bank	X -b	Equity	X
Deposits at ACH 2	+b +c		
Person 2			
Other assets	X	Equity	X
Car	-c		
Deposits at Bank 2	X +c		
Banknotes	X		
Central Bank			
Other assets	X	Deposits Bank 1	X -a
		Deposits Bank 2	X -b
		Banknotes	X
		Deposits TIPS	+a +b
		Equity	X

References

Atalay, E., Martin, A., & McAndrews, J. (2010). *Quantifying the benefits of a liquidity-saving mechanism*. FRB of New York Staff Report No. 447.

Bank of England. (2022). *CHAPS*. Available at: https://www.bankofengland.co.uk/payment-and-settlement/chaps

Bang-Jensen, J., & Gutin, G. (2007). Theory, algorithms and applications. *Springer Monographs in Mathematics*, Springer-Verlag London.

BdF. (2018). *Payments and market infrastructure in the digital age*. BdF Publication.

Bech, M. L., Preisig, C., & Soramaki, K. (2008). Global trends in large-value payments. *Economic Policy Review, 14*(2).

Bech, M. L., Shimizu, Y., & Wong, P. (2017). The quest for speed in payments. *BIS Quarterly Review*, March.

Bech, M. L., Hancock, J., & Zhang, W. (2020). Fast retail payment systems. *BIS Quarterly Review*, March.
Becher, C., Galbiati, M., & Tudela, M. (2008). The timing and funding of CHAPS Sterling payments. *Economic Policy Review, 14*(2).
Bindseil, U. (2019). *Central Banking before 1800: A rehabilitation*. Oxford University Press.
Bindseil, U. (2021). The future of central bank money: Digital currencies?. In Daniela Russo (Ed.) *Payments and market infrastructure two decades after the start of the European Central Bank* (pp. 290–302).
CPMI. (2016). *Fast payments – Enhancing the speed and availability of retail payments*. Bank of International Settlements.
CPMI. (2021). *Developments in retail fast payments and implications for RTGS systems*. Bank of International Settlements.
CPSS. (1997). Clearing arrangements for exchange-traded derivatives. Report prepared by the *Committee on Payment and Settlement Systems of the Central Banks of the Group of Ten Countries*, Bank of International Settlements, Basle.
CPSS. (2003). *The role of central bank money in payment systems*. Bank of International Settlements, Basle.
Davey, N., & Gray, D. (2014). How has the liquidity saving mechanism reduced banks' intraday liquidity costs in CHAPS?. *Bank of England Quarterly Bulletin*, Q2.
EBA Clearing. (2022a). *Single payments EURO1*. Available at: https://www.ebaclearing.eu/services/euro1/overview/
EBA Clearing. (2022b). *Instant RT1 payments - Overview*. Available at: https://www.ebaclearing.eu/services/rt1/overview/
EBA Clearing. (2022c). *Continuous gross settlement*. Available at: https://www.ebaclearing.eu/services/step2-t-system/settlement-continuous-gross-settlement-cgs/
ECB. (2019). *Card Payments in Europe – Current landscape and future prospects: a Eurosystem perspective*. European Central Bank.
ECB. (2021). *TARGET annual report 2020*. European Central Bank.
ECB. (2022a). *What is TARGET Instant Payment Settlement (TIPS)?*. Available at: https://www.ecb.europa.eu/paym/target/tips/html/index.en.html.
ECB. (2022b). *Successful completion of ACH migration to TIPS*. Available at: https://www.ecb.europa.eu/paym/intro/news/html/ecb.mipnews220328.de.html
Greene, C., Rysman, M., Schuh, S., & Shy, O. (2018). *Costs and benefits of building faster payment systems: The UK experience*. Working Paper Series No. 4. West Virginia University.
Martin, A., & McAndrews, J. (2008). Liquidity-saving mechanisms. *Journal of Monetary Economics, 55*(3), 554–567.
Norman, B. (2010). *Liquidity saving in real-time gross settlement systems*. Bank of England, Financial Stability Paper No. 7, May 2010.
The Clearing House. (2022). *About CHIPS*. Available at: https://www.theclearinghouse.org/payment-systems/chips.
Willison, M. (2004). *Real-time gross settlement and hybrid payment systems: A comparison*. Bank of England Working Paper No. 252.

Cross-Border Payments 5

5.1 Introduction

Payments across geographical distances have been taking place since the very beginning of economic activity Economic agents travel across regions in search of resources and vice versa. In tandem, goods are traded, and in many instances, are complemented with payments flowing in the opposite direction. It is in this sense that cross-border payments consist of transactions where the **payer and payee are located in different jurisdictions** (Bech et al., 2020). These also include instances in which payment flows between the payer and the payee are made offshore (Geva, 2013). Consequently, they are more complex than domestic payments as they involve multiple time zones and regulatory frameworks. Moreover, payments across borders can be in many instances facilitated through several intermediaries and a multitude of FMIs (CPMI, 2020; Bindseil and Pantelopoulos, 2022).

In parallel to domestic payments, cross-border flows can be broadly segregated into two subclasses. On the one hand, **cross-border retail payments** are typically small in terms of value. Examples include e-commerce, travellers using payment instruments from their home country, or remittances (like migrants sending money to their families at home) (CPMI, 2018b). Although cross-border retail payments consist of small-value transactions, they are generally of high-volume (Bank of England, 2021). Further, in recent years there has been a notable increase in the volume of cross-border retail transactions through Fintech intermediaries (e.g. Wise, Skirll, Revolut), which now complement other established Fintechs such as PayPal. On the other hand, **wholesale cross-border payments** are high-value transactions. Whilst large-scale international payment flows among commercial banks can be made on behalf of their clients (including for the purposes of settling retail payments), they can also take place between financial institutions on their own accord (see Chap. 7).

U. Bindseil, G. Pantelopoulos, *Introduction to Payments and Financial Market Infrastructures*, Springer Texts in Business and Economics,
https://doi.org/10.1007/978-3-031-39520-8_5

Another key distinction are cross border payments **with and without FX conversion**. For example, a US resident can transfer (i.e. remit) US dollars to a relative in India to be credited on the latter's account with an Indian Bank either denominated in USD or in Indian Rupees (assuming that the Indian bank offers also USD accounts to Indian residents). Also, an Indian resident could in principle transfer USD to a Pakistani resident, either across domestic accounts in the two countries, or through accounts in the US (if both have accounts in the USA). Most cross-border payments however include a FX conversion as residents typically hold domestic currencies in their accounts and have no ability or appetite to have accounts in foreign currency.

Irrespective of the type (i.e. retail or wholesale, with and without FX conversion), cross-border payments continue to be relatively complex, slow, expensive and opaque (CPMI, 2018b; FSB, 2020a). This is primarily due to a number of factors. As each payment and settlement system can only handle payments in the domestic currency, multiple entities can be involved in the settlement of a single cross-border transaction (Bech et al., 2020). Also, regulations such as anti-money laundering (AML), counter-finance terrorism (CFT) and know-your-customer (KYC) requirements must be adhered to across a multitude of jurisdictions, which add further complexities (CPMI, 2016a; Bank of Canada, Bank of England and Monetary Authority of Singapore, 2018).

For instance, in the case of large multinational companies or financial institutions, delays and the uncertainty about the timing of cross-border payments are important, whilst for smaller businesses and individuals, transaction fees are of primary concern. In particular, these challenges are exacerbated for end-users in emerging market and developing economies. McKinsey and Company (2018) estimate that a financial institution facilitating a cross-border payment will on average receive 20 US Dollars in fees from a single transaction. This is one of the reasons why Fintechs are increasing their market share as they are able to facilitate cross-border payments (e.g. remittances) at much more competitive rates (see e.g. Bindseil and Pantelopoulos, 2022).

The scale of payments being completed across borders are set to increase (KPMG, Bank of England and Monetary Authority of Singapore, 2018). Owing to an expansion of global trade and cross-border asset management, it is forecast that the value of international payment flows will accelerate from approximately 150 trillion US Dollars in 2017 to over 250 trillion by 2027 (Bank of England, 2021).

5.2 A Brief History of Cross-Border Payments and Their Universal Challenges

The process through which cross-border payments have been settled has evolved over the centuries (partially analogous to domestic payments, see Bindseil, 2019, 2021 and Russo, 2021). To some extent, medieval foreign trade and therefore cross-border payments were facilitated through the shipping of bullion, or via payment in gold coin (Einzig, 1962, 61–63). However, payment through coins was inconvenient, costly and time consuming, and in many cases, it was necessary to pay a professional "moneychanger" to ensure that the type and quality of any coins tendered were of the required standard (Mueller, 1997, Chap. 1; see also Kohn, 1999a).

The first major financial instrument employed for the purpose of executing international transactions was the **bill of exchange**, which came into being in the Arab world during the early Islamic era (Geva, 2011). As denoted by Kohn (1999b), the predominant function of bills of exchange was for remittance and trade finance, and provided a means of payment at a significantly lower cost than shipping bullion. In short, a bill of exchange was a written order by the issuer (drawer), which instructed a counterparty (drawee) to remit an amount, either immediately through a sight-bill or by a fixed date via a term-bill. If the drawee failed to pay (known as a "protest"), the drawer would be entitled to seek compensation through the courts, which would immediately execute an order against the failing party (Kahn et al., 2014; Bolton and Guidi-Bruscoli, 2021).

Prior to the First World War, global trade and cross-border payments had increased remarkably, ushering in the first era of globalisation (Keynes, 1919, 11). Whilst bills of exchange continued to be employed as an instrument of cross-border remittance, electronic direct deposit transfers through correspondent banking arrangements began in the second half of the nineteenth century after the laying of the first transatlantic cable (Eichengreen et al., 2021).

Although the use of telex messages for international interbank communication fundamentally increased the degree of financial integration, security and a lack of automation and standardisation remained an issue even in the post-war area (Köppel, 2011). As noted earlier, this prompted 239 banks from 15 countries to form a cooperative utility, the Society for Worldwide Interbank Financial Telecommunication (SWIFT), to reconcile problems in communicating across borders and to establish a common messaging standard. By the time SWIFT went live in 1977, 518 institutions from 22 nations were employing the SWIFT MT messaging standard (SWIFT, 2021a). SWIFT has recently announced that by November 2025, it will fully adopt the ISO 20022 messaging standard for all cross-border payments (SWIFT, 2021b).

Despite numerous evolutions, **many of the principal challenges associated with cross-border payments have been consistent across time**, as briefly summarised in Table 5.1. The list of frictions in cross-border payments shown in this table is largely based on FSB (2020a, 18–20). In addition, the measures considered currently by the G20 to address such frictions are outlined and structured in building blocks in FSB (2020b).

5.3 Correspondent Banking

The execution of cross-border payments can be explored in a fully developed correspondent banking model, **whereby payments are executed via complementary "nostro" and "vostro" accounts.** Although both nostro and vostro accounts

Table 5.1 Universal challenges of cross-border payments

	2020	1200–1900
1. Data standards and formats vary significantly	Adoption of new more comprehensive ISO20022 messaging format vs different insufficient legacy message formats (as supported in building block 14 of FSB 2020b).	Variety of conventions for example for the specification of bills of exchange. Handbooks like Kruse (1782) contain hundreds of pages explaining the different standards for coins and bills of exchange across global trade and settlement places.
2. Complex processing of compliance checks	AML/CFT and other compliance checks have been perceived as heavy by banks, also as their implementation across jurisdictions is heterogeneous, creating high costs and legal risks (discussed in building blocks 4–8 of FSB, 2020b).	Challenging compliance with usury prohibition in international bills of exchange in the Middle Ages and early modern times. See e.g. De Roover (1953).
3. Limited operating hours	If RTGS systems and correspondent banks have no overlapping opening hours, then the payment chain may be delayed awaiting the re-opening of a relevant system (covered in building block 12 of FSB, 2020b).	In the Middle Ages and in early modern times, documents or value tokens travelled slowly, so that daily operating hours per se did not matter. However, in case there were regular settlement days for bills of exchange (e.g. quarterly), then the combination of infrequent settlement days and slow travel of e.g. bills of exchange could lead to even longer settlement lags.
4. Legacy technology platforms	Payment systems may follow old standards and that are costly to modernise because they would require to be completely redone because of outdated standards or programming languages (building block 17 of FSB, 2020b explores the feasibility of new multilateral platforms for cross-border payments).	Technology per se was not a relevant category before the second half of the nineteenth century. Outdated standards and conventions could be classified as "legacy systems" but would be covered under 1.
5. Funding costs	Inefficient payment and settlement typically requires higher liquidity. Building block 11 of (FSB, 2020b) proposes liquidity bridges to address these challenges.	Interest rates and access to credit and thus the costs of liquidity were often significantly higher than today and therefore the need for liquidity in early trade was at least as pervasive as today.
6. Long transaction chains	Several correspondent banks may be needed in an international payment chain before settlement, delaying settlement and making it more expensive as each intermediary must be compensated (including for compliance related	Long payment chains were experienced with bills of exchange, which were often endorsed and passed on multiple times. However, this may also have been useful as in this way the bill could be used several times as a means of

(continued)

Table 5.1 (continued)

	2020	1200–1900
	work), making the chain less traceable and more opaque.	payment. The key trick of the bill of exchange was that all signatures in the chain of endorsements remained liable, so that the credit quality of a bill of exchange did not deteriorate when being passed on. On the other side that meant contingent liabilities for all signatories.
7. Weak competition	The high costs and risks associated with AML/CFT regulation and fines applied to banks led to a withdrawal of many banks from this business ("de-risking"), providing the remaining actors more market share and thus pricing power.	Cross-border payments were often dominated by relatively few internationally active banking houses (like the Fuggers, Medicis, or later the Rothschilds). As a result, these banking houses were able to gain market power and accumulate significant wealth.
8. Crime threat	Cyber-risk management creates significant costs and entry barriers and is perceived to be an increasing challenge and cost factor for any bank, payment system and market infrastructure.	Physical extortion of value token, robbery (both in transport and in vault) etc. Reduced significantly through a reliance on bills of exchange.
9. Slow speed and high costs of shipment	Hardly relevant today as costs of international data transmission have collapsed over the last decades.	Highly relevant in the past when value tokens or paper credit had to travel physically over long distances.
10. Relevance and challenges of currency conversion	International payments are typically done in international currencies, implying local currency conversion relying on banks offering such services at a cost to the end user (taken up in building block 13 of FSB, 2020b).	Numerous coin types and qualities circulating in parallel. Heterogeneous coinage and Gresham's law as major driver of reliance on paper instruments and the emergence of early commercial and public giro banking.

have different names, they represent the identical account when viewed from the perspective of each bank (King, 2010, 53). Through the introduction of correspondent banking, one bank (the correspondent) provides a service to another bank (the respondent) (CPMI, 2016a; ***ECB, 2016b). The Wolfsburg Group (2014, 1) outlines that "correspondent banking is the provision of a current or other liability account, and related services, to another financial institution . . . used for the execution of third party payments and trade finance, as well as its own cash clearing, liquidity management and short-term borrowing or investment needs in a particular currency." Correspondent banking relationships underpin remittance, international trade and serve as a means for executing humanitarian monetary flows across economies. Consequently, they also play a crucial role in fostering financial development and stability (The World Bank Group, 2018). The evolution of correspondent banking has recently found renewed interest in academic research, with the Oxford University launching a major research project on correspondent banking in the period 1870 to 2000 (Schenk, 2021 being the first publication of this project).

To depict the most rudimentary form of such arrangements, suppose there are two large multinational banks (Bank A and Bank B), which are located in different nations (nation A and nation B). If one adopts the point of view of Bank A, any deposits held at Bank B are recognised as assets on its balance sheet within its **nostro account ("our account with you")**, and is denominated in foreign currency. Thus, any nostro account balances are a claim by Bank A on Bank B. As Harfield (1951, 436–437) puts it, "[f] oreign exchange, as . . . conducted by banks, is not a dealing with money . . . It is, rather, a dealing in credit, accomplished by bookkeeping entries and not by transfer of tangible property . . ." Taken from the perspective of Bank B, the identical account is the **vostro account ("your account with us")**, which is denominated in local currency and is held as a liability. As denoted by De Roover (1944, 385), ". . . most of the time vostro accounts. . . [have] . . . a credit balance representing money held on deposit [o] n behalf of a foreign principal."

From the perspective of the respondent bank, nostro account balances require careful management. The bank needs to reduce the chance of incurring any overdrafts so as to avoid hitting overdraft limits or incurring interest costs (King, 2010, 72–73). But since payment and settlement systems across the globe have different operating hours, it is difficult to always identify the exact balance within a nostro account throughout the course of the day (Hudson, Colley and Largan, 2000, 50). Indeed, failure to properly account for inflows and outflows of deposits can lead to an array of problems and can cause liquidity risks to be amplified, leading to the bank incurring overdraft charges in order to complete a payment (King, 2010, 70).

Often a single intermediary (typically a large financial institution) may be employed for the purposes of completing any cross-border transactions between two banks that are located in different jurisdictions. This may transpire when a cross-border payment is denominated in a currency which differs from either the payer or the payee, and thus refers to a **loro account ("their account with you")**.

Correspondent banking is becoming increasingly concentrated among a small number of large institutions (***ECB, 2016; Rice et al., 2020). This is predominantly owing to the requirement to comply with several layers of regulations (IMF, 2017, 1). Consequently, respondent banks are now inclined to only conduct their business in a handful of correspondent banks, rather than through a multitude of service providing banks, known as "de-risking". Moreover, correspondent banks have often reduced the number of currency corridors they serve. Accuity (2017) estimate that the number of correspondent relationships for cross-border payments denominated in US Dollars has fallen by 15% since 2013. Similarly, there has been a 23% decline since 2009 for international transactions denominated in euros.

In the instance of a cross-border payment through correspondent banking (in which the payment is invoiced in the domestic currency of the payee), the bank of the exporter debits the vostro account of the importer's bank, and also credits the deposit account of the exporter, which allows purchased goods to be received. In this way, whilst the importer is able to maintain a deposit account in local currency, the exporter is able to receive payment in the respective domestic currency. Any cross-border payments are typically counterbalanced through each bank granting the other respective bank a cross-border interbank loan. According to Kumhof et al. (2020, 30), "... when the bank receives the deposit, this does not give it any additional funds ... Instead it automatically lends the funds the instant it receives them." This signifies that the balance of payments remains equilibrated, as any current account deficit (surplus) is exactly offset by a financial account surplus (deficit), the latter due to an increase (decrease) in cross-border claims.

The classical application of correspondent banking is to effectuate a transfer of deposits in the instance where traders engage in the purchase of goods Consider the following steps below where payments are completed between two large financial institutions that have an established direct bilateral relationship. Note that for simplicity, we assume that all steps take place more or less simultaneously.

- Trader A from country A imports real goods from country B for an amount of "a" that is invoiced in currency B and is therefore worth "βa" in A-currency. β is the number of **currency A units** required to purchase **1 unit of currency B**.
- Trader A instructs their bank, Bank A, to transfer the funds to the account of Trader B, the exporter located in B-country who has their account with Bank B. Bank A debits the deposit account of Trader A. Bank B debits the vostro account of Bank A and credits the deposit account of Trader B.

Aside from direct bilateral relationships, there exist a multitude of other avenues through which cross-border payments may be completed. Typically, arrangements will be dependent on the size of the payer and payee's financial institutions. In the event that small regional banks execute international transactions on behalf of their clients, then **one or several large global banks may act as intermediaries.** This is shown below, where an analogous transaction is considered to the one depicted above in Table 5.2 (again, for simplicity we assume that all transactions occur simultaneously). We assume that two large internationally active banks act as intermediaries between two small domestic banks which serve the non-bank clients (i.e. the importer and the exporter). In both countries, the domestic settlement between the large and small banks is done via the central bank RTGS system (i.e. in central bank money).

Typically, **only relatively few banks will for every currency act as correspondent banks**. Let's assume that we have two currencies with two banking systems of 1000 banks each. Then, suppose there could be in each currency five correspondent banks, with each of them having nostro/vostro accounts with the five correspondent banks in the other currency, i.e. in total 10 bilateral correspondent banking relationships. For example, the 1000 banks in country A need each to choose one of the five large correspondent banks in country A to transmit their cross-border orders (via the foreign correspondent bank, i.e. the five large banks in country B).

Table 5.2 Cross-border payments with a direct bilateral relationship

Country A - in A currency			
Trader A (importer)			
Real goods	X +βa	Equity	X
Deposits	X -βa		
Bank A (large internationally active bank)			
Deposits at central bank	X	Deposits	X -βa
Nostro with B	X -βa	Vostro B	X
		Equity	X
Country B - in B currency			
Bank B (large internationally active bank)			
Deposits at central bank	X	Deposits	X +a
Nostro with A	X	Vostro A	X -a
		Equity	X
Trader B (exporter)			
Real goods	X -a	Equity	X
Deposits	X +a		

Two forces will determine the number of banks in correspondent banking. On the one hand, holding nostro accounts with foreign banks is expensive from a credit risk and regulatory capital perspective. Being attractive for foreign banks' nostro accounts (i.e. the bank's own vostro accounts) also requires a good reputation and scale, and an excellent credit rating, which requires large amounts of (expensive) capital. On the other hand, this is a large market which may generate attractive fee income in particular since the market is oligopolistic.

One may wonder where the FX conversion takes place in correspondent banking, as obviously the payment cases represented in the above financial accounts include a currency conversion from the currency of the importer into the currency of the exporter. Actually, in the examples above, no FX market operation takes place. Bank A (in Table 5.2) and Bank A2 (in Table 5.3) just accept a change in their cross-currency (and cross-border) positions that occur through changes in the correspondent banking accounts which compensates for the trade imbalance (meaning that once again the balance of payments is equilibrated). Therefore, these banks (i.e. Bank A and Bank A2 in Tables 5.2 and 5.3, respectively) have provided FX conversion services as part of providing their correspondent banking services.

In sum, **correspondent banking will continue to be subject to two main drawbacks**. First, even in the instance where payments can be completed instantaneously, existing claims and liabilities in respective nostro and vostro accounts will continue to be denominated in commercial bank money, thereby potentially posing financial stability risks. It will continue to rely on a complex network of claims and liabilities ("IOUs" between banks) which are not cleared regularly with one single medium of exchange. At the same time, banks tend to be well-supervised everywhere, and they typically benefit—as long as they remain solvent—from a lender of

Table 5.3 Cross-border payments with intermediaries

Country A - in A currency			
Trader A (importer)			
Real goods	X **+βa**	Equity	X
Deposits	X **-βa**		
Bank A1 (small bank)			
Deposits at central bank	X **-βa**	Deposits	X **-βa**
Other assets	X	Equity	X
Bank A2 (large internationally active bank)			
Deposits at central bank	X **+βa**	Deposits	X
Nostro with B2	X **-βa**	Vostro B2	X
		Equity	X
Central Bank A			
Other assets	X	Deposits Bank A1	X **-βa**
		Deposits Bank A2	X **+βa**
		Banknotes	X
		Equity	X
Country B – in B currency			
Central Bank B			
Other assets	X	Deposits Bank B1	X **+a**
		Deposits Bank B2	X **–a**
		Banknotes	X
		Equity	X
Bank B2 (large internationally active bank)			
Deposits at central bank	X **–a**	Deposits	X
Nostro with A2	X	Vostro A2	X **-a**
		Equity	X
Bank B1 (small bank)			
Deposits at central bank	X **+a**	Deposits	X **+a**
Other assets	X	Equity	X
Trader B (exporter)			
Real goods	X **-a**	Equity	X
Deposits	X **+a**		

last resort (LOLR). Also, settlement in commercial bank money is not per se problematic, at least not for low-volume cross-border payment corridors.

Second, while being less vulnerable to the abuse of market power and/or fragmentation related to closed-loop solutions (e.g. Fintechs, bitcoin, stablecoins), **it is still by nature an approach which has been and will continue to be significantly concentrated amongst a few participants**. Correspondent banking benefits from network effects, in which the large players can offer better services than small players. This will continue to prevail even if some banks return to offering correspondent banking services because of lower compliance costs and risks. Nonetheless, dominant correspondent banks will inevitably exploit their market power through higher than competitive fees.

5.4 Correspondent Banking as a Solution for Domestic Payments?

Correspondent banking is not a good solution for domestic payments Assume that there are four banks in nation A (Bank A1, Bank A2, Bank A3 and Bank A4). To avoid a reliance on central bank money (or in the absence of a central bank), the four banks can become credit-interconnected by lengthening their balance sheets through granting each other vostro/nostro accounts (with an initial value of "a") for the purposes of completing deposit transfers on behalf of their customers (for an amount **b**, **c**, and **d**) (Table 5.4):

Although it may appear that there is no longer any need for a centralised monetary authority for the settlement of payments, such a "multilateral domestic corresponding banking approach" suffers from some drawbacks, as there is an extensive build-up of "IOUs" between the participants. In the context of domestic payments, this has been overcome through the introduction of central banking, as in holding risk-free IOUs in the form of deposits at the central bank, the necessity for

Table 5.4 Correspondent banking for domestic payments

Country A - in A currency			
Bank A1			
Nostro with A2	+a	Deposits	X -b
Nostro with A3	+a -b	Vostro A2	+a
Nostro with A4	+a	Vostro A3	+a
		Vostro A4	+a
		Equity	X
Bank A2			
Nostro with A1	+a	Deposits	X +c +d
Nostro with A3	+a	Vostro A1	+a
Nostro with A4	+a	Vostro A3	+a -c
		Vostro A4	+a -d
		Equity	X
Bank A3			
Nostro with A1	+a	Deposits	X +b -c
Nostro with A2	+a -c	Vostro A1	+a -b
Nostro with A4	+a	Vostro A2	+a
		Vostro A4	+a
		Equity	X
Bank A4			
Nostro with A1	+a	Deposits	X -d
Nostro with A2	+a -d	Vostro A1	+a
Nostro with A3	+a	Vostro A2	+a
		Vostro A3	+a
		Equity	X

banks to maintain some form of IOU structure in lower credit-quality IOUs is averted (i.e. all participants accept a novation of claims).

In the example above with n = 4 banks, there will be "n(n − 1)/2" bilateral IOU relationships (or "n(n − 1)" if one counts all the correspondent accounts if there is no bilateral netting). For 10 banks this means 45 bilateral net exposures, for 100 banks 4950, etc. In an international context, this inflation of bilateral bank exposures is avoided by having only few large banks specializing in correspondent banking. The same could be done of course also domestically and this would indeed reduce the number of bilateral relationships. However, the price would be concentration and market power of the banks serving as central hubs, and eventually a single public domestic "correspondent bank" should emerge as a solution: the (public) central bank offering (vostro) accounts to all domestic banks.

The drawbacks associated with a multilateral domestic corresponding banking approach can be exemplified by examining the arrangements in Venice before the introduction of the Banco di Rialto in 1587 (see e.g. Bindseil, 2019, 207) or in the context of the United States during the nineteenth century. James (1978, 95–97) notes that prior to the US Civil War, many banks began to deposit funds in several leading trade centres, such as in New York City. Under conditions "knowledge and confidence", respondent banks universally accepted the IOUs of correspondent banks (James and Weiman, 2010). Indeed, New York City banks acted as correspondents to such an extent that by 1850 they completed payments on behalf of 600 banks across the United States. This was replicated in Chicago, as by 1868 banks acted as correspondents to financial institutions in Illinois, Iowa and Wisconsin. However, others, such as Colwell (1859, 628), began to put forward that some form of centralised authority was necessary to reduce the fragilities associated with a multilateral system of correspondent banks:

> When the banking system of this country, the power and efficacy of which for public advantage cannot be denied, whatever may be its equally undeniable abuses and perversions, is to be superseded, whether for the special benefit of the public treasury, or form commercial considerations, this inquiry must be not how to introduce coins, but how to find a substitute for banks, or how to secure the facilities of banking without its mischiefs.

As a second-best solution to that of a central bank, Colwell (1859, 271) proposed that correspondent banking relations be concentrated in large commercial centres:

> [T]he banks in the West may fall largely in debt to those of the East for goods purchased for Western consumption ... The result of these bank accounts, and the correspondence by which they are kept up, is the same as if they all had a common clearing-office, at which each should be debited and credited with all they had to pay, and all they had to receive.

Following the National Banking Acts of 1863 and 1864, a three-tiered banking system structure was founded through (1) central reserve city banks, (2) reserve city banks and (3) country banks. At the top of the pyramid, central reserve city banks in New York, Chicago and St. Louis were required to maintain a 25% reserve against deposits and notes in circulation (Meltzer, 2003, 78–79). Acceptable forms of reserves included gold or gold certificates, with the latter issued to the public as a substitute for gold coins, thus constituting an alternative form of banknote (Simmons, 1936). In turn, a 25% cover ratio was also imposed on reserve city banks, half of which could be held at central reserve city banks. Finally, a 15% minimum reserve requirement was enforced for country banks, of which 9% could be held as deposits in reserve or central reserve city banks (James, 1978, 98; see also James and Weiman, 2010).

But during instances of financial panics and crises, many country banks recalled a proportion of or all of their deposits with correspondent banks (Gibbons, 1864, 359). In acting as the focal point for the national banking system, central reserve city banks in New York were therefore often forced to suspend payments during the panics of 1804, 1857, 1890 and 1893 (James, 1978, 120). With the domestic financial system lacking a credible LOLR, news of financial distress amplified across the nation. For instance, in the financial crisis of 1857, Gibbons (1864, 357) explains that "[d]uring the week of financial excitement, in October last, the exaggerated reports of which were carried with the speed of light lightning to every part of the land, this new medium of communication (the telegraph) filled our banks with imperative orders for the immediate return of . . . deposits, in specie." It is in this sense that it becomes readily evident as to why correspondent banking is not a universal solution for domestic payments.

5.5 Cross-Border Payment Fintechs Present in Multiple Countries

What we call cross-border payment Fintechs tend to be e-money institutions or payment services providers more or less specialised in cross-border payments These include both broad retail payment services providers like PayPal (which has so far not been very ambitious in terms of offering cheap cross-border retail payment services) and various newer, smaller companies rapidly building up a customer base, such as Wise, Skrill, Revolut and others. The reason for the high efficiency of Fintechs entering the retail cross-border payment market may relate to their (i) lean set up (e.g. no branches; only internet access; fresh organisational set up); (ii) specialisation (compared to e.g. universal banks); (iii) possibly lighter regulatory treatment; (iv) innovative technologies; and (v) their aggressive market entry to gain a customer base. In contrast to stablecoins, Fintechs do not pretend that e.g. a reliance on DLT or blockchain are crucial to their transfer and settlement model, and actually do not seem to apply such technologies.

The legal type (bank, e-money institution, etc.) of a Fintech will of course depend on the frameworks available in the jurisdictions in which they operate. Often these would be treated as specialised payment services providers or e-money institutions with a lighter regulation than banks in view of the absence of risky assets and an assumed matching of payment liabilities with very low risk and fully liquid assets.

The settlement mechanics of Fintechs offering retail cross-border payments are not necessarily identical, and one Fintech covering various currencies may also have established different settlement arrangements in different countries, without this necessarily making an obvious difference to customers. **On the payer side**, at least two options would be possible:

- The payer needs to establish an account with the Fintech provider and must first load funds to the account via a direct debit of their bank account or through a transfer of funds from it. Then the payer can trigger a payment up to the pre-funded amount.
- Under a second option, the payer triggers a fund transfer in one go together with the cross-border payment order, e.g. through a fast payment order, that is triggered by the Fintech through an application programming interface (API) allowing the Fintech to act as a payment initiator with the consent of the payer. This is more efficient for the user but requires open banking and an instant payment system.

On the payee side, again different options would be possible:

- First, the payee receives a notification via email or text message that they are receiving a payment via a Fintech platform and that they need to register first before the receipt of the payment is possible. If already registered, then the payment can come in directly into their bank account. This approach has the advantage that the payer does not need to know nor need to reveal to the Fintech the bank account details of the payee (as a very minimum, the payer just needs to know the "proxy", which is the email address or the phone number of the payee). Only the payee would have to provide them to the Fintech if they are willing to accept the payment via this channel. Two sub-cases exist: the payee needs to register with their bank account details and the money once coming in is directly paid into their bank account. Alternatively, the money is only transferred on the account of the payee with the Fintech, and then the payee needs to trigger the transfer to any bank account (e.g. their own bank account or that of someone else).
- Alternatively, the payee could directly receive the payment in their bank account (without ever registering with the Fintech), but this requires that the payer knows and registers correctly all the bank details and other relevant information of the payee with the Fintech.

In both currency areas, the Fintech may or may not have a banking licence or other ways to access central bank money. If it does not have an account with the central bank, it would use instead a commercial bank account. In the following example below, we assume that the Fintech has in the country of the payer (country A) a license giving it access to central bank money while in the country of the payee (country B), it has only a commercial bank account (it could obviously be the other way around, or any of those on both sides). We also assume that the payee is already

Table 5.5 Instant cross-border payment through a Fintech payment services provider

Country A - in A currency			
Household A			
Account Fintech Account Bank A	X +βa1 -βa2 X -βa1	Equity	X -βa2
FintechX – subsidiary A			
Deposits at central bank	X +βa1	Deposits Household A Liab. FintechX – sub. B	X +βa1 -βa2 X +βa2
Bank A			
Deposits at central bank	X -βa1	Deposits Account Household A	X X -βa1
Central Bank A			
Other assets	X	Deposits Bank A Deposits FintechX sub. A	X -βa1 X +βa1
Country B - in B currency			
Household B			
Deposit FintechX-B Deposits Bank B2	X +a2 –a3 X +a3	Equity	X +a2
FintechX subsidiary B			
Deposits with Bank B1 Claim on FintechX – sub. A	X -a3 X +a2	Deposit Household B	X +a2 -a3
Bank B1			
Deposits at central bank	X -a3	Deposits FintechX B	X -a3
Bank B2			
Deposit at central bank	X +a3	Deposits Household B	X +a3
Central Bank B			
Other assets	X	Deposit Bank B1 Deposit Bank B2	X -a3 X +a3

Table 5.6 Consolidated account of the Fintech

FintechX consolidated view - in B currency			
Deposits at central bank (A) Deposits at Bank B1	X +a1 X -a3	Deposits Household A Deposits Household B	X +a1 -a2 X +a2 -a3

registered, and that the money is paid in and out in both currencies through instant payments (including in the payer's currency through an API). We assume that the payment is a remittance and that the value to be received in B currency is "a". Moreover, we assume that the payment stays on the account of the Fintech in both countries only for a few moments, but enough to show it in the accounts below. Therefore, we can think of **a1, a2, a3** as occurring sequentially all say in less than an hour, in line with what the best Fintechs achieve according to the World Bank tracker (see https://remittanceprices.worldbank.org) (Table 5.5).

It is useful to recall that FintechX is in fact one global company, i.e. one can take a consolidated approach to its balance sheet, which would be as follows under the model where funds are first loaded on the accounts of households with the Fintech. We assume moreover that the holding company is in B-country and therefore has accounts in B-currency (Table 5.6).

5.6 Global Stablecoins

The most ambitious global stablecoin initiative so far, Libra/Diem, claimed in its 2019 white paper to aim at providing an ethical, inclusive, frictionless, low-cost global payment network for all As a construct, Diem was envisaged to offer (in its White Paper 2.0 version) both single currency coins, and a composite coin based on the IMF-SDR currency basket (called "≋LBR"). Both would be fully backed by highly liquid assets. The Libra Reserve—i.e. the assets to match the issued stablecoin—was envisioned to be composed essentially of high-quality liquid assets (e.g. government bonds).

In what follows below, we consider the financial accounts representation of payments in the following two cases: **(i) without FX conversion using a global stablecoin denominated in any reference asset** (such as a currency basket, a single currency, or a commodity); and **(ii) using two separate single currency stablecoins which however are part of one global network** (like single currency stablecoins envisaged by Diem).

(i) **Without FX conversion (i.e. a single stablecoin used globally for payments).** In many ways, it does not really matter what assets are underpinning the stablecoin—it could be a basket of global securities, a single currency, or gold etc. Country B is the exporter of a good that has a price in the domestic currency "a". The price expressed in the global stablecoin is "αa" (where α is the number of stablecoin units needed to buy one unit of B-currency). The price expressed in the currency of A-country is βa (β is the number of A-currency units needed to buy one B-currency unit; needless to say that arbitrage implies that one needs α/β units of the stablecoin to buy one unit of the A-currency) (Table 5.7).

Table 5.7 Stablecoin used without FX conversion

Country A - in A currency			
Firm (or household) A			
Real goods	X **+βa**	Equity	X
Bank deposits	X		
Stablecoin	X **-βa**		
Global stablecoin (e.g. in SDR basket)			
Res. (e.g. Gvt bonds)	X	SC owned by firm A	X **-αa**
		SC owned by firm B	X **+αa**
		SC held by others	X
Country B – in B currency			
Firm (or household) B			
Real goods	X **-a**	Equity	X
Stablecoin	X **+a**		
Bank deposits	X		

Table 5.8 Two stablecoins denominated in domestic currencies with FX conversion

Country A - in A currency			
Firm (or household) A			
Real goods	X +**βa**	Equity	X
A-Stablecoin	X -**βa**		
Bank deposits	X		
A-stablecoin (in A currency)			
Reserve	X -**βa**	SC owned by firm A	X -**βa**
		SC held by others	X
Country B – in B currency			
B-stablecoin (in B currency)			
Reserve	X +**a**	SC owned by firm B	X +**a**
		SC held by others	X
Firm (or household) B			
Real goods	X -**a**	Equity	X
B-Stablecoin	X +**a**		
Bank deposits	X		

Table 5.9 Case (ii)

Investor (in any place)		
Country B bonds	X + **a**	Equity X
Country A bonds	X − **a**	

(ii) **With FX conversion (i.e. two domestic stablecoins denominated in the respective fiat currency)** (Table 5.8).
The cross-border payment seems to take place without the creation of any cross-border claim(s). However, if one would consider the full financial accounts, and would look for what is implied by the change of the reserve of the stablecoin in both currencies, one realizes that there has to be a counterbalancing item that squares the accounts on both sides. For example, some investor in country A, B or a third country, has to switch from A-bonds into B-bonds, as shown below (Table 5.9).

When one includes this account, then the domestic accounts in each country balance.

Because of their flexibility, stablecoins have the **potential to provide an efficient means of cross-border payment for several reasons:**

- First, stablecoins can be rather efficient as they are per se technology agnostic, i.e. the most efficient and modern technology can be chosen.
- Second, low costs can also be achieved thanks to scale, e.g. in case existing membership in social networks is used as a basis to onboard users. Indeed, BigTechs like Facebook with billions of customers can approach potential stablecoin customers efficiently, even if additional KYC is required for payment functions to prevent illicit payments and money laundering, particularly in an international context.

- Third, by binding their value to existing fiat currencies or to related meaningful baskets like the SDR, the value stability required for a means of payment can be achieved.

There are however some potential drawbacks of stablecoins, which include:

- A successful global stablecoin which would perform well in terms of universal reach would have significant market power across international borders, presumably giving it leeway to eventually exploit this market power in one way or another. BigTechs could also store, use and sell payments data, raising privacy concerns (see e.g. Adachi et al., 2020; FSB, 2020c; Panetta, 2020; CPMI-IOSCO, 2021).
- International regulators and standard setters have identified significant potential financial stability and market integrity issues relating to the large-scale balance sheet of a global stablecoin and its reserve of liquid assets. In case of a massive sell-off of stablecoins by holders, the need of the stablecoin vehicle to liquidate assets is likely to destabilise markets, implying fire sale losses. This could only be prevented if the stablecoin invests exclusively into the most liquid and risk-free assets, and/or has adequate equity buffers. Any surveillance on how the strablecoin issuer manages these reserves is not straightforward to design and implement, also from a legal perspective, depending also on the regulatory framework of the licensing country. Relatedly, it is unclear who would provide a lender-of-last resort function to a global stablecoin issuer.
- The cross-border usage of global stablecoins (including cross-border holdings) implies significant risks of currency substitution and of related macro-economic destabilisation. This can be limited by allowing only cross-border use involving FX conversion between stablecoins denominated in the two relevant domestic currencies.
- Successful global stablecoins will likely be perceived by sovereign states as a threat to their monetary sovereignty. In addition to the issue of currency substitution, the availability of global cross-border payment information to the stablecoin issuer and its use for commercial purposes, or access to it by a foreign power, and the possible vulnerability of the stablecoin issuer to political pressures (e.g. sanctioning initiatives suddenly prohibiting to serve certain jurisdictions), create vulnerabilities for nation states and their citizens.

5.7 Interlinking Domestic Payment Platforms with a Competitive FX Conversion Layer

CPMI (2018a) explains that whilst interconnecting domestic payment infrastructures for the settlement of cross-border payments is complex, it may have significant advantages, relative to innovative closed-loop solutions. The basis for interlinking instant payment systems in a cross-border context is the rise of domestic instant payment platforms in many jurisdictions around the globe, as already noted by

CPMI (2016b). Instant (or "fast") payments are payments in which the transmission of the payment message and the availability of final funds to the payee occur in real time or near-real time and as close to a 24/7 basis as possible. The creation of bilateral or multilateral arrangements—through interlinking payment systems—and integrating an instant FX conversion layer—would in principle allow for cross-currency/cross-border payments to be completed in central bank money. A number of preconditions however need to be fulfilled for this:

- **Addressability of accounts cross-border:** ideally, there is a global standardization of unique bank account identifiers (such as the IBAN) to ensure an efficient and secure routing of the payment to the payee. The Single European Payment Area (SEPA) has achieved this for the adhering European countries. From the user perspective, addressing accounts via a proxy (e.g. a unique e-mail address or a unique phone number) would be advantageous, but would require a global proxy-look up solution.
- **Interlinking:** The two or more instant payment systems need to be interlinked through a connecting layer that transmits payment orders from one domestic system to the other and more generally routes payment process information in both directions. This layer needs to address possible differences in message data formats by providing translation capabilities, while ideally being cost efficient.
- **An instantaneous and cost-efficient currency conversion layer:** This layer would effectively decompose the (pseudo-) cross-border payment into two domestic instant payments. Market makers would consist of banking groups having accounts in instant payment systems on both sides i.e. in the two relevant domestic instant payment systems. The cross-border payment would therefore be "simulated" by the banking group providing the FX conversion service, as one member of this group would simultaneously receive a payment in currency A by the payer (located in country A) within the country A domestic instant payment system, and the other member of the banking group, namely the one in B country would make in currency B a domestic instant payment to the payee within the domestic instant payment system of country B. To ensure that the currency conversion layer maintains an instant processing of the cross-border payment, market makers would have to accept an obligation to provide immediately executable, binding quotes for cross-currency payments up to the agreed maximum value. The automated process would always immediately choose the most attractive conversion rate amongst the provided binding bid-ask quotes. The set up should incentivize a sufficient number of banks to commit to be FX market makers in the conversion layer, such as to ensure competitive price setting, depth and liquidity. This will of course be simpler for large FX/cross-border payment corridors.
- **Straight-through processable instantaneous AML/CFT checks:** Finally, AML/CFT compliance checks should be made automated and instantaneous by relying on positive ex ante criteria. Of course, "suspicious" payments would have to be rejected or be re-routed to a non-instant processing to allow for additional non-automated analysis.

The settlement mechanics involve the following steps:

- Firm A purchases a good from Firm B for a value of "a" in B-currency.
- It pays via an instant payment in A-currency with its bank, Bank A. The banking app of Bank A is able to convert for Firm A the amount of currency that it needs to transfer from its A-currency account with Bank A to be an equivalent amount when converted into B-currency. This relies on the cross-border FX conversion layer selecting amongst market makers the best quote for the currency A to currency B conversion. This happens to be FXBank which is a banking group that has subsidiaries in both currency regions. The FX conversion quote is "β" (for simplicity we assume that the real good's value is also calculated in the same manner in the accounts of Firm A).
- Settlement of the FX transaction effectively consists of two domestic instant payment credit transfers between bank accounts with the central bank on each side, whereby the market maker (FXBank) acts as counterparty on both sides and creates as a balancing item an intra-FXBank group claim and liability. This illustrates that in some sense "cross-border payments with FX conversion" do not really exist.
- To achieve PvP, settlement needs to be simultaneous, and must be linked through the relevant program code (Table 5.10).

There are a number of advantages of interlinking domestic instant payment systems through a competitive FX conversion layer, as also developed in the BIS Innovation Hub's Nexus report (BISIH, 2021):

- **It is efficient** as it re-utilizes the domestic instant payment infrastructure and the associated services of banks and their relationship with bank account holders (including KYC).
- **It preserves competitiveness** to the extent that the connecting and conversion layer is not run by a single profit-maximizing firm with market power but governed like a utility which aims at organizing strong competition between FX market makers. Further, it also avoids the potential market power of closed-loop stablecoin arrangements and/or the implied market fragmentation.
- Compared to correspondent banking, **it allows for a simpler, more efficient and more competitive architecture** of cross-border payments.
- It preserves the **universal reach** achieved by correspondent banking (every bank account holder can be addressed if a link has been established).
- **Monetary sovereignty is preserved** as interlinking prevents currency substitution and the global power of a few dominant payment firms (such as under a global stable coin arrangement).

Potential challenges relate to the technicalities and costs of interlinking and setting up the competitive and instantaneous currency conversion layer, which requires willingness and ability to collaborate not only by network service providers and message standard setters (e.g. SWIFT, ISO 20022) but also by legislators and central

Table 5.10 Instant cross-border payment with central FX conversion layer

Country A (in A currency)			
Firm A			
Real goods	X +βa	Equity	X
Account Bank B	X -βa		
Bank A			
Dep. at central bank	X -βa	Deposits	X -βa
Other assets		Credit central bank A	X
		Equity	X
Central Bank A			
Credit to banks	X	Deposits Bank A	X -βa
		Deposits FX Bank A	X +βa
		Banknotes	X
		Equity	X
FX Bank – A-country subsidiary			
Dep. at central bank	X +βa	Cred. central bank A	X
Other assets	X	Intra-Group liability	X +β a
FX Bank – B-country subsidiary			
Dep. at central bank	X -a	Cred. central bank B	X
Intra-Group claims	X +a		
Other assets	X		
Country B (in B currency)			
Firm B			
Real goods	X -a	Equity	X
Account Bank B	X +a		
Bank B			
Dep. at central bank	X +a	Deposits	X +a
Other assets	X	Credit central bank B	X
		Equity	X
Central Bank B			
Credit to banks	X	Deposits Bank B	X +a
		Deposits FX Bank B	X -a
		Banknotes	X
		Equity	X

banks, i.e. there needs to be a political will to remove possible barriers and to make the arrangement legally sound, also in contingency scenarios, such as the default of a party to a payment. In other words, the legal and political set up costs have to be added to the other fixed costs of such arrangements.

Interlinking will probably not be a solution for very narrow cross-border payment corridors in which the costs of the interlinking will be relatively high, and where it will be difficult to organize sufficient competition within the FX conversion layer, also in view of liquidity costs for the FX conversion services providing banks. A key element of the efficiency of interlinking will be the width of the bid-ask spread on which users can rely. This width will depend on factors such as (i) volatility of exchange rate; (ii) cost and reliability of liquidity available to FX conversion service providing banks in both currencies; (iii) duration for which a quote needs to remain binding (in view of processing times in the payment initiation phase).

Notwithstanding these various challenges, it seems that for more important corridors the interlinking of domestic instant payment systems can constitute the "holy grail" of cross-border payments: it appears efficient, relies on existing tested and successful infrastructures, and avoids closed loop systems and the associated fragmentation and potential abuse of market power, whilst preserving monetary sovereignty. Global initiatives like Nexus could reduce the set-up costs for individual payment corridors by realizing economies of scale on the technical side and by providing a benchmark for domestic system providers and legislators.

5.8 How Will Cross Border Payments Progress Further?

Cross border payments would ideally be **(1) immediate, (2) cheap, (3) universal in terms of reach, and (4) settled in a secure settlement medium such as central bank money** (Bindseil and Pantelopoulos, 2022). It could be achieved thanks to the rapid decline in the costs of global electronic data transmission and computer processing, new payment system technology (allowing for instant payments), innovative concepts (such as the interlinking of payment systems including a currency conversion layer), and unprecedented political will and global collaboration like the G20 work on enhancing cross-border payments.

Stablecoins, traditional correspondent banking, and cross-border Fintechs can all contribute to progress towards better cross-border payments. From a public policy perspective, stablecoins appear somewhat more problematic than the other two options as they tend to be closed loop solutions, leading thereby to fragmentation, and if successful may abuse their market power. The interlinking of domestic instant payment systems with a competitive FX conversion layer may have the highest potential to deliver the holy grail for larger cross-border payment corridors as they combine (i) technical feasibility; (ii) relative simplicity in their architecture; and (iii) maintaining a competitive and open architecture by avoiding the dominance of a small number of market participants who would eventually exploit their market power. Moreover, (iv) monetary sovereignty is preserved, and (v) the crowding out of local currencies is avoided due to a FX conversion layer at the border (which does not hold for global stablecoins). Interlinking of domestic payment systems would also perform well in terms of preserving the universal reach of correspondent banking (although of course only for the payment areas that are actually interlinked). Finally, all solutions require that strong progress is made on the AML/CFT compliance side to ensure straight-through processing for the large majority of cross-border payments.

References

Accuity. (2017). *Derisking and the demise of correspondent banking relationships, a research report by Accuity*. RELX Group.

Adachi, M., Cominetta, M., Kaufmann, C. & van der Kraij, A. (2020). *A regulatory and financial stability perspective on global stablecoins*, ECB Macroprudential Bulletin, No. 10, 5 May 2020.

Bank of Canada., Bank of England., & Monetary Authority of Singapore. (2018). *Cross-border interbank payments and settlements, emerging opportunities for digital transformation*.

Bank of England. (2021). *Cross-border payments*. Available at: https://www.bankofengland.co.uk/payment-and-settlement/cross-border-payments

Bank of International Settlements Innovation Hub (BISIH). (2021). *Nexus – A blueprint for instant cross-border payments*. Bank of International Settlements.

Bech, M. L., Faruqui, U., & Shirakami, T. (2020). Payments without borders. *BIS Quarterly Review*, March.

Bindseil, U. (2019). *Central Banking before 1800: A rehabilitation*. Oxford University Press.

Bindseil, U. (2021). The future of central bank money: Digital currencies?. In Daniela Russo (Ed.) *Payments and market infrastructure two decades after the start of the European Central Bank* (pp. 290–302).

Bindseil, U., & Pantelopoulos, G. (2022). *Towards the holy grail of cross-border payments*. European Central Bank Working Paper Series No. 2693.

Bolton, J., & Guidi-Bruscoli, F. (2021). 'Your flexible friend': The bill of exchange in theory and practice in the fifteenth century. *The Economic History Review*.

Colwell, S. (1859). *The ways and means of payment: A full analysis of the credit system, with its various modes of adjustment*. J. B. Lippincott & Co.

CPMI. (2016a). *Correspondent banking*. Bank of International Settlements.

CPMI. (2016b). *Fast payments – Enhancing the speed and availability of retail payments*. Bank of International Settlements.

CPMI. (2018a). *Central bank digital currencies*. Bank of International Settlements.

CPMI. (2018b). *Cross-border retail payments*. Bank of International Settlements.

CPMI. (2020). *Enhancing cross-border payments: Building blocks of a global roadmap. Stage 2 report to the G20*. Bank of International Settlements.

CPMI-IOSCO. (2021). *Consultative report. Application of the Principles for Financial Market Infrastructures to stablecoin arrangements*, October 2021.

De Roover, R. (1944). Early accounting problems of foreign exchange. *The Accounting Review, 19*(4), 381–407.

De Roover, R. (1953). *L'évolution de la lettre de change, XIV-XVIIIième siècles*, Paris, A. Collin.

Eichengreen, B., Ferrari, M. M., Lafarguette, R., & Mehl, A. (2021). *Technology and the geography of the foreign exchange market*. NBER Working Paper No. 21884.

Einzig, P. (1962). *The history of foreign exchange*. Macmillan.

FSB. (2020a). Enhancing cross-border payments, stage 1 report to the G20.

FSB. (2020b). Enhancing cross-border payments, stage 3 roadmap.

FSB. (2020c). Regulation, supervision and oversight of 'Global Stablecoin' arrangements, 13 October 2020.

Geva, B. (2011). *The payment order of antiquity and the middle ages: A legal history*. Bloomsbury Publishing.

Geva, B. (2013). Global payment and settlement systems. In *Handbook of key global financial markets* (pp. 513–522) Institutions and Infrastructure.

Gibbons, J. S. (1864). The Banks of New York, their dealers, the clearing house and the panic of 1857. Appleton & Co.

Harfield, H. (1951). Elements of Foreign exchange practice. *Harvard Law Review, 64*(3), 436–444.

Hudson, R., Colley, A., & Largan, M. (2000). *The capital markets and financial management in banking*. Global Professional Publishing.

International Monetary Fund. (2017). *Recent trends in correspondent banking relationships – Further considerations*. International Monetary Fund.
James, J. A. (1978). *Money and capital markets in postbellum America*. Princeton University Press.
James, J. A., & Weiman, D. F. (2010). From drafts to checks: the evolution of correspondent banking networks and the formation of the modern US payments system, 1850–1914. *Journal of Money, Credit and Banking, 42*(2–3), 237–265.
Kahn, C., Quinn, S., & Roberds, W. (2014). Central banks and payment systems: The evolving trade-off between cost and risk. In *Norges Bank conference on the uses of central banks: Lessons from history*.
Keynes, J. M. (1919). *The economic consequences of the peace*. Macmillan and Co.
King, M. J. (2010). *Back office and operational risk: Symptoms, caused and cures*. Harriman House.
Kohn, M. (1999a). *Early deposit banking. Working Paper 99–03*, Dartmouth College.
Kohn, M. (1999b). *Bills of exchange and the money market to 1600*. Working Paper 99–04, Dartmouth College.
Köppel, J. (2011). *The SWIFT affair: Swiss banking secrecy and the fight against terrorist financing*. Graduate Institute Publications.
Kruse, J. (1782). *Allgemeiner und besonders Hamburgischer Kontorist Welcher von den Währungen, Münzen, Gewigten, Maassen, Wechsel-Arten und Usanzen der vornehmsten in und ausser Europa gelegenen Städte und Länder*. 4th edition, 2 volumes.
Kumhof, M., Rungcharoenkitkul, P., & Sokol, A. (2020). *How does international capital flow?* Bank of England Staff Working Paper No. 884.
McKinsey and Company. (2018). A vision for the future of cross-border payments. *Global Banking Practice, 2018*.
Meltzer, A., & H. (2003). *A history of the federal reserve, volume 1: 1913–1951*. University of Chicago Press.
Mueller, R. C. (1997). *The Venetian money market: Banks, panics, and the public debt, 1200–1500*. JHU Press.
Panetta, F. (2020). *The two sides of the (stable)coin, Speech delivered at Salone dei Pagamenti*, 4 November 2020, published on ECB website.
Rice, T., von Peter, G., & Boar, C. (2020). On the global retreat of correspondent banks. *BIS Quarterly Review*, March.
Russo, D. (ed.). (2021). *Payments and market infrastructure two decades after the start of the European Central Bank*. ECB Publication.
Schenk, C. R. (2021). The development of international correspondent banking in the USA 1970–1989. *Global Correspondent Banking 1870–2000 Working Paper Series*, Vol. 1, No. 1, University of Oxford.
Simmons, E. C. (1936). The gold certificate. *Journal of Political Economy, 44*(4), 534–543.
SWIFT. (2021a). *SWIFT history*. Available at: https://www.swift.com/about-us/history
SWIFT. (2021b). *ISO 20022 adoption programme*. Available at: https://www.swift.com/standards/iso20022/iso-20022-programme/timeline
Wolfsburg Group. (2014). *The Wolfsberg anti-money laundering principles for correspondent banking*. Wolfsberg Banking Principles.
World Bank Group. (2018). *The decline in access to correspondent banking services in emerging markets: Trends, impacts, and solutions lessons learned from eight country case studies*. The World Bank Group.

Central Counterparties 6

6.1 Introduction

A central counterparty (CCP) interposes itself to derivatives contracts traded between counterparties, be it privately negotiated contracts—**over the counter (OTC) derivatives**—or those which are traded on a public exchange (**exchange traded derivatives**). Examples of OTC traded derivatives are **forwards and swaps.** Exchange traded derivatives are typically composed of **options and futures.** In all of these cases, a bilateral trade is struck between two parties regarding when a particular agreement will be settled at some point in the future (i.e. at T + t). The merits of CCPs for the efficiency and stability of financial markets had been recognised prior to the Global Financial Crisis. For example, CPSS-IOSCO (2004, 1) summarised the benefits of CCPs as follows:

> A CCP has the potential to reduce significantly risks to market participants by imposing more robust risk controls on all participants and, in many cases, by achieving multilateral netting of trades. It also tends to enhance the liquidity of the markets it serves, because it tends to reduce risks to participants and, in many cases, because it facilitates anonymous trading. However, a CCP also concentrates risks and responsibility for risk management in the CCP. Consequently the effectiveness of a CCP's risk controls and the adequacy of its financial resources are critical aspects of the infrastructure of the markets it serves.

Prior to the Global Financial Crisis, **OTC derivative markets** however **rarely relied on any centralised trading mechanism,** while exchange traded derivatives were already cleared via CCPs (Thomadakis & Lannoo, 2021). In this way, individual traders in OTC derivatives were generally reliant on relatively few dealers with whom they had signed credit support documentation to protect against credit risk (e.g. Merrill Lynch, Goldman Sachs, BNP Paribas, Citigroup, JP Morgan Chase) (Ruffini & Steigerwald, 2014).

Although the centralised clearing of contracts has been practiced for at least 130 years (see below), regulatory frameworks received renewed emphasis following

U. Bindseil, G. Pantelopoulos, *Introduction to Payments and Financial Market Infrastructures*, Springer Texts in Business and Economics,
https://doi.org/10.1007/978-3-031-39520-8_6

the Global Financial Crisis, which revealed the complex network of OTC derivative exposures between major financial institutions (Domanski et al., 2015). In response, at the 26 September 2009 summit in Pittsburgh, G20 leaders agreed that all standardised OTC derivative contracts should be cleared through CCPs by the end of 2012 and that OTC derivative contracts should be reported to trade repositories. Consequently, for both the European Union and the United States, it is now stipulated that all standardised OTC contracts be cleared through CCPs, as legislated by the **European Market Infrastructure Regulation (EMIR)** and the **Dodd-Frank Act**, respectively. This, however, does not mean that clearing through CCPs was not identified as an important topic prior to crisis, as noted above (see also CPSS-IOSCO, 2004; ECB, 2007; Mallaby, 2016, 349–351).

For some CCPs, clearing services are only offered for one type of financial instrument (mono-product clearing), whereas other CCPs clear multiple financial instruments (multi-product clearing) (e.g. exchange-traded derivatives and OTC derivatives) (BdF, 2018, 169). Typically, larger CPPs will clear a multitude of instruments, whereas smaller CCPs clear one type of financial instrument. Participants of a CCP are recognised as **clearing members** and must meet minimum credit standards (Council of Financial Regulators, 2011).

6.2 Key Activities of CCPs

From the perspective of counterparties involved in any bilateral agreement, it is beneficial to rely on a CCP when managing margin calls due to fluctuations in the price of the underlying asset. For instance, the **buyer of say a futures contract takes a "long" position** and will profit if the value of the asset rises. In contrast, **the seller of the contract incurs a "short" position**, and profits if the value of the asset decreases. Should the value of the asset increase (decrease), the seller (buyer) of the contract is required to pay a **variation margin** to the respective counterparty, reflecting **mark-to-market** changes in the value of the contracts. This by definition **generates a series of post-trade claims and liabilities denoting that parties to the trade become credit-interconnected.**

The interposition of CCPs offers some unique advantages. Through **novation, post-trade claims are concentrated on the CCP**, and the CCP becomes the buyer to every seller, and the seller to every buyer, thereby ensuring the performance of open contracts (Garvin, 2012; Domanski et al., 2015). This requires that the CCP is fully trusted by all in the sense that every party considers the liabilities of the CCP to be at least as good as the liabilities of other traders, stipulating that the novation of a claim towards the CCP is always accepted. In this way, IOU networks can be netted away (see e.g. Bindseil and Pantelopoulos, 2022). This holds even if extended to an infinite number of parties (Council of Financial Regulators, 2011). Hence, the imposition of the CCP reduces direct **credit-interconnectedness and improves financial instability**, as through its risk management framework, CCPs provide an assurance to creditors that all claims will be fulfilled (Gregory, 2014, 6).

Table 6.1 Symmetric and asymmetric exposure matrix.

Liabilities↓ Claims →	1	2	3	4	5	Total Assets
1		1	1			2 (0)
2	(1)		1	1		2 (1)
3	(1)	(1)		1	1	2 (2)
4	1 (1)	(1)	(1)			2 (3)
5	1 (1)	1 (1)	(1)	(1)		2 (4)
Total Liabilities	2 (4)	2 (3)	2 (2)	2 (1)	2 (0)	

The first clearing house for the clearing of contracts was established in the United States by the Chicago Board of Trade in 1883. Still, this clearing house did not interpose itself as a CCP, as there was no novation of contracts. It was only in 1925 that the Chicago Board of Trade formed the Board of Trade Clearing Cooperation and interposed itself between counterparties through novation (Moser, 1994; Kroszner, 2006). It is likely that the first clearing house that interposed itself through novation for the clearing of contracts—thereby acting as a true CCP—would have emerged in the late nineteenth century in commodity exchanges in both Germany and France (Bliss & Papathanassiou, 2006; BdF, 2018, 165). In Germany, the exchanges of Hamburg (Coffee), Magdeburg (Sugar) and Leipzig were one of the first to establish themselves as CCPs. As Emery (1896, 71–72) puts it:

> The coffee trade in Europe seems to have developed a special form of clearing-house known as the caisse de liquidation or Liquidationskasse, which has also been adopted in a few cases by grain exchanges. The peculiarity of this form is that the clearing-house itself becomes responsible on all contracts. When the parties first make a contract, notice is given . . . and a deposit made for security. In case of the default of either party the clearing-house secures the other party to the contract from loss, and makes its own account good, so far as possible, from the assets of the defaulting party . . . [In turn] . . . [t]he caisse de liquidation is in reality a party to each contract. All payments are made to it and all deliveries are made by it.

To demonstrate why novation towards a CCP is useful, consider an exposure matrix of 5 parties as shown below in Table 6.1, whereby all bilateral post-trade claims and liabilities have a value of 1. These post-trade claims and liabilities could be due to the **price of the underlying asset changing,** and hence, participants that have incurred liabilities are required to **post a variation margin**. The first example is symmetric in the sense that each party posts a total of two claims whilst also incurring a total of two liabilities. In contrast, in the asymmetric example (in parenthesis), some of the parties are only debtors (party 1), others only creditors (party 5), while the remaining parties are mixtures of varying degrees between the two. Only party 3 in the middle is equally a creditor and a debtor, analogous to the symmetric example.

Both the symmetric **(unbroken arrows)** and asymmetric examples **(broken arrows)** can be represented through digraphs. For instance, in the symmetric

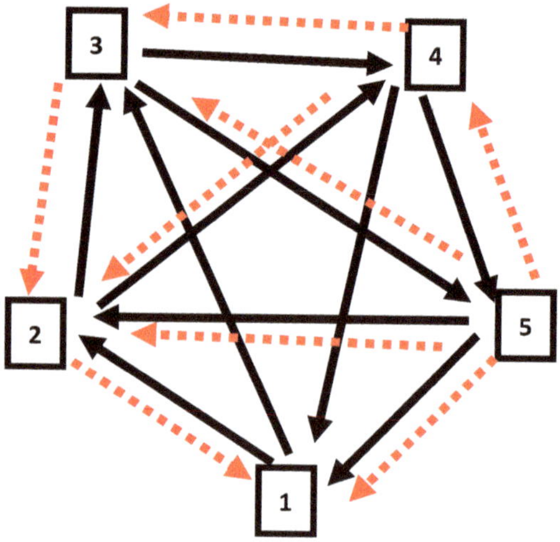

Fig. 6.1 Symmetric and asymmetric exposure matrix

example, party 3 posts a claim on party 5. Therefore, the unbroken black arrow originates at party 3, and terminates at party 5. Since in the asymmetric example party 1 does not post any claims on other parties, no arrows originate from party 1. On the flipside, as party 5 posts a total of 4 claims, four broken arrows originate from it (Fig. 6.1).

Without clearing through a CCP, an uncleared OTC derivative trade would imply a lasting credit relationship in which the net value of bilateral derivative trades between two parties would be subject to bilateral collateralisation agreements—such as those stipulated by a ISDA credit support annex (CSA)—which defines the terms for the provision of collateral by the parties of the derivatives trade. While initial margin was normally not foreseen, variation margins were required, i.e. whenever the value of the contracts fluctuated, collateral positions were adjusted in a way to preserve protection. This implied the necessity to sign a high number of CSAs and to manage protection via collateral with a high number of counterparties on a day-to-day basis.

Whilst bilateral netting can certainly mitigate the amount of collateral required for credit protection, such solutions are fairly limited relative to the potential of central clearing and hence the novation of contracts in two predominant ways: (1) counterparty risks are substantially reduced, and (2) there is a larger scope for netting.

In the context of liquidity efficiency in RTGS systems (Chap. 4, Sect. 4.2), we noted that every circle of payment obligations in a payment system can be eliminated through an appropriate mechanism. In the context of financial contracts, the existence of a CCP can be considered to be such a mechanism. Since all parties have equal claims on one another in the **symmetric** example, the external circle can therefore be eliminated. What remains is also actually also a circle, which becomes obvious if one were to change the order of the parties. All obligations can therefore be netted away without any residual financial exposures. On the other hand, the potential for netting is far less reaching in the **asymmetric** example, given that no

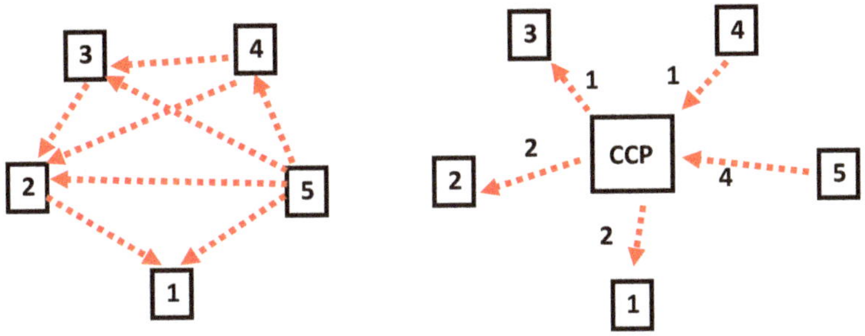

Fig. 6.2 Asymmetric exposure matrix

credit circle is identifiable (left hand side of Fig. 6.2). However, some multilateral netting of post-trade claims continues to be possible, resulting in some parties incurring liabilities (parties 1 and 2) to the CCP and other traders posting claims (parties 4 and 5) on the CCP (right hand side).

6.3 Risk Management Framework for CCPs

As novation is at the core of the CCP business model, financial risk management is crucial for CCPs (Carter & Garner, 2015). It is indeed imperative that the CCP operates under a robust risk management framework, as a CCP will typically face both current and potential risk exposures. As denoted by CPSS-IOSCO (2012, 41–42), **current exposures** arise as a consequence of past fluctuations in the market value of the underlying asset. On the other hand, **future exposures** develop from the potential for the market value of the underlying asset to suddenly change, which can thereby expose the CCP to a defaulting participant (see also Murphy and Vause, 2021).

From its point of view, the CCP is equipped with **several layers of defence**—often denoted as a **"default waterfall"**—via its risk management scheme to cover any losses if a clearing member were to default on its obligations (CPMI-IOSCO, 2017). Should this transpire, the CCP "... deploys a cascade of tools and measures to make its activities as secure as possible in the face of any conceivable market crisis" (Norman, 2011, 10).

The **first line of defence** is that prior to the novation of contracts, the CCP requests collateral from participants, generally via securities or cash (Duffie et al., 2015). If collateral is provided through securities, the CCP will typically apply a valuation haircut. Analogous to the collateralised lending operations of the central bank, the size of the haircut will be dependent on the quality of the asset pledged (for an extensive discussions on collateral and valuation haircuts, see e.g. Nyborg, 2017; Barthélemy et al., 2018).

Two types of margin need to be distinguished: **(1) initial margin deposits** and **(2) variation margins**. The **initial margin deposit**, or initial margin, is deposited with the CCP. The initial margin corresponds to the estimated loss that the CCP will be required to cover over a short time horizon (generally 5 days) prior to the liquidation of collateral, after the default of a participant (Priem, 2018). From the perspective of the CCP, it is presumed that the size of the initial margin will be large enough to cover any shortfalls even under the presence of adverse market conditions, with e.g. a 99% probability (Huang & Takáts, 2020; Hull, 2012). Typically, CCPs apply **portfolio margining,** whereby the initial margin amount is based on an estimate of the losses of a clearing member's overall portfolio, including across different instruments. Through portfolio margining, the CCP can request (significantly) lower initial margins from clearing members than if initial margins had been calculated instrument by instrument and/or on a currency-by-currency basis.

While initial margin (as the name implies) must be posted to the CCP by clearing members at the outset of the post-trade process, **variation margins** are designed to protect the CCP following market prices fluctuating of the outstanding derivate positions, in principle in the same way as it applied to bilateral non-cleared derivative positions collateralised within the framework of an ISDA CSA. For instance (as denoted above), should the value of the derivatives portfolio of a clearing member be negative from the member's perspective, then the member needs to provide an amount of collateral that covers this negative position. Through **marking-to-market** and daily **margin calls**, the CCP can account for changes in the value of trades on its books, and is therefore contains its exposure to market risk (Elliot, 2013). Should market volatility be high, margin calls will be made even at multiple times during the course of the day.

There is one important difference between initial and variation margins initial margins are only posted one way, by clearing members to the benefit of the CCP, while for variation margins the CCP does not have a privileged, asymmetric position, but collects from, and posts to collateral in an ex ante symmetric way with its counterparties. Moreover, different patterns of price changes will have different effects on the two types of margin. A gradual but in cumulated terms significant change of market prices over say 3 months can significantly increase variation margins but will have moderate effects on initial margins. In contrast, a temporary extreme volatility, say with prices being extremely volatile within 1 week but then returning largely to their previous levels, will lead to strong and lasting increases of initial margins, but not to lasting increases of variation margin. The duration of the increase of the initial margin will depend on the time horizon of the volatility model of the CCP.

In case of negative tail events, a CCP may still incur a loss if the defaulting member's initial margin were to be insufficient. To fulfill its responsibilities and prevent its own default, the CCP must therefore be equipped with an adequate stock of additional resources. To this end, clearing members of the CCP must therefore also contribute to a **default fund, which acts as a second line of defence for the CCP**. As with initial margins, the methods for calculating the contributions of clearing members to the default fund are determined by the CCP, typically in

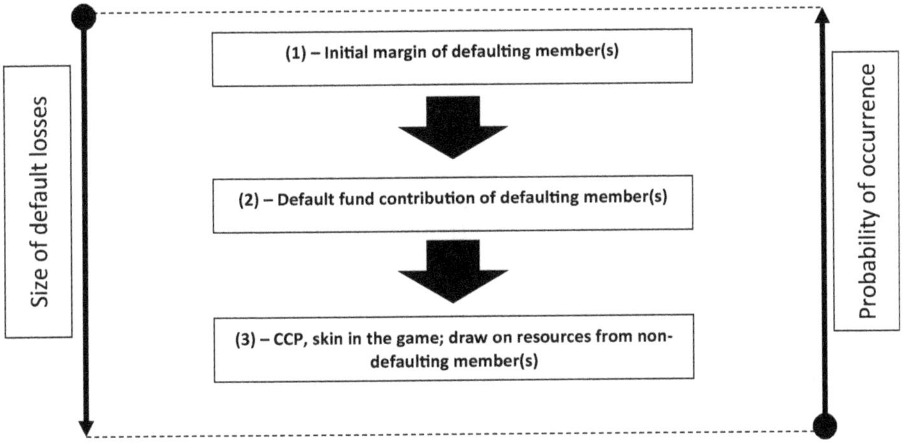

Fig. 6.3 The default waterfall

approximate relation to the level of risk that the participant beings to the CCP (Elliot, 2013), in conjunction with the CCPs own internal stress tests (Eurex, 2019). As a minimum, CCPs must at least cover the default of the participant with the largest exposures (Cover 1). For more systemically important CCPs—or those which clear complex products—coverage is more stringent, as it is envisaged the CCP will cover the defaults of two participants with the largest exposures (Cover 2) (CPMI-IOSCO, 2017).

Should the first two lines be broken, the CCP can then contribute its own resources by drawing down on its own capital, often denoted as **skin in the game** (Domanski et al., 2015). In addition, **a CCP can also draw on the resources of non-defaulting members** through (i) accessing their default fund contributions, and (ii) may even request for supplemental funds from surviving members (BdF, 2018, 179–180). Therefore, in enacting its **third line of defence**, the CCP has a loss-absorbing capacity which is beyond the constraints of its balance sheet (Faruqui et al., 2018). This nonetheless does not preclude a CCP from defaulting on its obligations, as although they have been rare, three CCPs have failed in recent history (see e.g. Cross, 2021).

In terms of liquidity , central banks often are ready to act as a lender of last resort to the CCP (see e.g. Cœuré, 2019). For instance, in the United States, the Federal Reserve in line with the Dodd-Frank Act can provide additional liquidity to distressed CCPs in times of extreme market stress. Likewise, the Bank of England can in certain circumstances intervene as a lender of last resort to stressed CCPs (Bank of England, 2022). In the euro area, some CCPs have banking licenses and therefore can take recourse to the regular marginal lending facility (Fig. 6.3).

In conjunction with the default waterfall, an additional risk protection measure of CCPs is to set stringent criteria for **direct membership** of clearing members or CCP participants. Generally, criteria are based on publicly observable characteristics, such as credit ratings published by rating agencies, and mainly relate to the scope of the participant's business, its status, and its solvency. Like other FMIs, CCPs often have a tiered membership, with direct participants and indirect ones, who are clients of the direct participants. However, **indirect participation** models need to ensure that risks relating to indirect members are contained. This raises the issue of the segregation of positions, which is a risk management issue for both the CCP and its client (CSPP-IOSCO, 2012, 84–85). **Indirect participation** can be achieved via an **individual account structure** in which each individual indirect participant's collateral is held in a separate, segregated account at the CCP. In an **omnibus account structure,** collateral belonging to all customers of a particular direct participant is pooled ("commingled") and held in a single account. Whilst such an approach can be operationally more efficient, it might create risks.

Because of the significant efficiency gains of concentration of clearing with few CCPs resulting from portfolio margining approaches, the clearing of derivatives are concentrated in a handful of CCPs (Faruqui et al., 2018). To this end, Coeure (2019) highlights that for many CCPs in the EU, the vast majority of derivatives cleared are instigated by participants outside the CCP's home member state. Consequently, these CCPs can be exposed to bankruptcies in multiple regions, which poses the need for measures to mitigate the threat of systemic risk (Gregory, 2014, 54). Moreover, the global use of CCPs raises the question of regulatory recognition of foreign CCPs for the use by domestic banks and the prudential implications. For example, the EU has designed within EMIR 2.2 a progressive and risk-driven approach to the recognition of third-country CCPs (TC-CCPs). A TC-CCP established in a third country may only provide clearing services to clearing members and trading venues established in the Union, if that TC-CCP is recognised by the European Securities Market Authority (ESMA). Recognition is dependent on the European Commission adopting a so-called "equivalence decision" for the third-country's legal, supervisory and enforcement framework in relation to CCPs. Moreover, ESMA needs to have concluded cooperation arrangements or Memoranda of Understanding (MoU) with the relevant authorities to support supervisory cooperation and information exchange. ESMA publishes a list of TC-CCPs—in April 2023, 39 TC-CCPs were included in this list. Cooperation arrangements have been signed with authorities from 22 countries, implying that the 39 TC-CCPs were in as many jurisdictions. Foreign authorities apply similar frameworks towards EU CCPs.

6.4 Financial Account Illustration of Central Clearing Through CCPs

To depict the central clearing of contracts, the financial accounts below illustrate the case of a derivative (e.g. futures) contract cleared with a CCP. In this example, both clearing members are direct members of the CCP. Note that the accounting treatment of derivatives and of the posting of margins is in practice complex and changes are normally not displayed in official financial accounts as suggested below. What is

Table 6.2 Domestic clearing through a single CCP

Country X – in X currency			
Clearing Member 1			
Deposits at central bank	X **-d** -b -a2	Other liabilities	X
Default fund contrib. to CCP	**+d**	Equity	X -a1
Margin posted to CCP	+b +a2		
Net value of portfolio	-a1		
Other assets	X		
CCP			
Deposits at central bank	**+2d** +2b +a2 -a2	Initial margin	+2b
Other assets	X	Default fund	**+2d**
		Variation margin CM1	+a2 -a2
		Equity	X
Clearing Member 2			
Deposits at central bank	X **-d** -b +a2	Other liabilities	X
Default fund contrib. to CCP	**+d**	Equity	X +a1
Margin posted to CCP	+b -a2		
Net value of portfolio	+a1		
Other assets	X		

shown below is more of an economic interpretation of the flows of funds and equity impacts.

- When the CCP was established, the clearing members had to **contribute to the default fund**, each for an amount "d", which was settled in central bank money.
- At T + 0, two clearing members agree to the terms of the contract (e.g. price, duration etc.). The contract is cleared with the CCP and the CCP imposes **initial margins** "b" on the clearing members. The two clearing members transfer the initial margin to the CCP, this being settled in central bank money (note that d > b).
- Suppose that at T + t the spot price of the underlying asset falls. As a result, clearing member 1—which holds a long position—incurs a capital loss "a1" which on the asset side is recorded in a position called below called "net value of derivatives position". On the flipside, clearing member 2 posts a capital gain of "a1", as it holds a short position.
- The CCP issues a **variation margin** call in the amount of "a2" that will be settled on T + 1 to clearing member 1, whilst clearing member 2 gets a variation margin pay-out of the same amount by the CCP. Again, these variation margins are settled in central bank money (note that a1 = a2) (Table 6.2).

6.5 Performance of CCPs in Times of Market Stress

One heavily discussed issue with CCPs is that they could potentially contribute to the pro-cyclicality of the financial system (Brunnermeier & Pedersen, 2009; Murphy et al., 2014; Glaser & Panz, 2016). In times of extreme market stress, CCPs will generally demand larger initial margins, may increase haircuts and even limit collateral eligibility (King et al., 2020; Benos et al., 2022). In turn, cascading asset prices will result in higher variation margin calls by CCPs (Bakoush et al., 2019). To meet such demands, stressed participants could then be forced into asset fire sales, which may result in asset prices declining further, creating a viscous circle of downward asset price volatility (European Systemic Risk Board, 2020) and systemic liquidity risks (Murphy & Vause, 2021). At the same time, **it has also been noted that CCPs will normally decrease the risk of procyclicality, primarily for two reasons.** First, by decreasing counterparty risks, CCPs may avert complete gridlock and ensure that trades in derivatives continue. Second, the use of centralised multilateral netting minimises the degree to which collateral must be posted (thereby reducing the extent of asset fire sales etc.) (Cecchetti et al., 2009; see also Financial Stability Board, 2020). That CCPs improve financial stability is not questioned, as the procyclicality of margining is at least as relevant for non-cleared contracts.

The effectiveness of CCP risk management schemes during periods of extreme market stress was somewhat evident with the advent of the Global Financial Crisis (Wendt & Shabsigh, 2015). Bell and Holden (2018) denote that CCPs proved to be fairly resilient following the Lehman Brothers default. In clearing contracts for Lehman Brothers, Monnet (2010) describes that the London-based CCP LCH. Clearnet was exposed by around $9 trillion, which encompassed a total of 66,390 trades across five major currencies. However, LCH. Clearnet managed to liquidate all of Lehman's portfolio without recourse to the default fund. It is for such reasons that Norman (2011) describes CCPs as the "unlikely heroes" of the Global Financial Crisis.

The Covid-19 pandemic also tested the resilience of CCP risk management schemes Huang and Takáts (2020) and CPMI-IOSCO (2021) convey that market volatility culminated in large price movements, prompting significant margin calls from CCPs in terms of both initial and variation margins. Initial margins increased because of the significant increase of volatility (in a forward-looking sense), while variation margins increased because of the large changes in values of cleared derivative contracts that had materialised. Indeed, in some instances, initial margin requirements doubled for many exchange-traded derivatives (Murphy & Vause, 2021). This strained the liquidity positions of clearing members, who—for those which were not equipped with high-quality liquid assets (HQLA) on their balance sheets—began to hoard liquid assets in anticipation of larger initial margin and variation margin calls. In spite of substantial market turbulence, CCPs withstood the turmoil relatively unscathed (Financial Stability Board, 2020). Nonetheless, according to ISDA (2021), there were three cases where clearing member defaults did culminate in some minor disruptions, with two rectified via the use of default funds, whilst the third was remedied without recourse to default funds. Heeding the lessons of the Covid-19 pandemic, ISDA (2021) has suggested that "forward looking" and "conservative" margin requirements be adopted so as to ensure that any increases in margin in response to market volatility are less severe (see also CPMI-IOSCO, 2021).

CPMI-IOSCO (2022) is the final report on CCP margining with respect to the market turmoil of March 2019. It provides a detailed analysis of changes of initial and variation margins. According to the report (see p. 2), daily CCP variation margin calls increased from around $25 billion to a peak of $140 billion. The total initial margin requirement across CCPs increased by roughly $300 billion during March 2020, with a further increase in excess collateral posted of $115 billion, resulting in an overall increase in collateral prepositioned at CCPs of $415 billion (an approximate 40% increase relative to the average in February 2020). Slightly less than half of this collateral was held in cash.

In a similar vein, the **2022 Russian invasion of the Ukraine** sparked large upward swings in commodity prices (in particular power and gas), generating large variation margin calls from CCPs for those participants with a short position (McCrank, 2022; Mourselas, 2022) as well as large initial margin increases for all in view of the unprecedented volatility in these markets. Nonetheless, ESMA (2022) reports that aside from one low-value default from a direct clearing member, negative impacts on CCPs were contained.

Aside from periods of widespread market turmoil, **the risk management schemes of CCPs have also been required to manage the defaults of participants on several other occasions**. Such instances include when a clearing member of KRX CCP defaulted in South Korea in 2013, and in 2018 when the Stockholm based OMX CCP experienced the default of a clearing member (Bell & Holden, 2018; Ewald et al., 2022).

References

Bakoush, M., Gerding, E., & Wolfe, S. (2019). Margin requirements and systemic liquidity risk. *Journal of International Financial Markets, Institutions and Money, 58*, 78–95.

Bank of England. (2022). *SMF operating procedures*. Available at: https://www.bankofengland.co.uk/-/media/boe/files/markets/sterling-monetary-framework/operating-procedures

Barthélemy, J., Bignon, V., & Nguyen, B. (2018). *Monetary policy and collateral constraints since the European debt crisis*. Banque De France Working Paper No. 669.

BdF. (2018). *Payments and market infrastructure in the digital age*. BdF Publication.

Bell, S., & Holden, H. (2018). Two defaults at CCPs, 10 years apart. *BIS Quarterly Review*, December 2018.

Benos, E., Ferrara, G., & Ranaldo, A. (2022). *Margin procyclicality and the collateral cycle*. Bank of England Staff Working Paper No. 966.

Bindseil, U., & Pantelopoulos, G. (2022). *A brief history of payment netting and settlement*. IBF Paper Series 01-2022.

Bliss, R. R., & Papathanassiou, C. (2006). Derivatives clearing, central counterparties and novation: The economic implications. *Central Counterparties and Novation: The Economic Implications (March 8, 2006)*.

Brunnermeier, M. K., & Pedersen, L. H. (2009). Market liquidity and funding liquidity. *The Review of Financial Studies, 22*(6), 2201–2238.

Carter, L., & Garner, M. (2015). Skin in the Game–Central Counterparty Risk Controls and Incentives. *RBA Bulletin*, June, 79–88.

Cecchetti, S. G., Gyntelberg, J., & Hollanders, M. (2009). Central counterparties for over-the-counter derivatives. *BIS Quarterly Review*, September.

Cœuré, B. (2019). *The case for cooperation: Cross-border CCP supervision and the role of central banks. Introductory remarks by Benoît Cœuré, Member of the Executive Board of the ECB, at a conference on CCP risk management organised by the Deutsche Bundesbank, the ECB and the Federal Reserve Bank of Chicago*, Frankfurt am Main, 27 February 2019.

Council of Financial Regulators. (2011). *Central clearing of OTC derivatives in Australia*. Australian Prudential Regulation Authority, Australian Securities and Investments Commission, Reserve Bank of Australia and the Department of the Treasury, Commonwealth Government, Australia.

CPSS-IOSCO. (2004). *Recommendations for central counterparties*. Bank of International Settlements.

CPMI-IOSCO. (2017). *Resilience of central counterparties (CCPs): Further guidance on the PFMI*. Bank of International Settlements.

CPMI-IOSCO. (2021). *Consultative report. Application of the Principles for Financial Market Infrastructures to stablecoin arrangements*, October 2021.

CPMI-IOSCO. (2022). *Review of margining practices*. Bank of International Settlements.

CPSS-IOSCO. (2012). *Principles for financial market infrastructures*. Bank of International Settlements.

Cross, N. (2021). Examining the causes of historical failures of central counterparties. *RBA Bulletin*, June Quarter 2021.

Domanski, D., Gambacorta, L., & Picillo, C. (2015). Central clearing: Trends and current issues. *BIS Quarterly Review*, December.

Duffie, D., Scheicher, M., & Vuillemey, G. (2015). Central clearing and collateral demand. *Journal of Financial Economics, 116*(2), 237–256.

ECB. (2007). The role of central counterparties. Issues related to central counterparty clearing, *ECB-FED Chicago Conference*, 3–4 April, 2006.

Elliot, D. (2013). *Central counterparty loss-allocation rules*. Bank of England Financial Stability Paper No. 20.

Emery, H. C. (1896). *Speculation on the stock and produce exchanges of the United States*. Columbia University.

Eurex. (2019). *Spotlight on: CCP risk management*. Eurex Clearing AG.

European Securities and Markets Authority. (ESMA). (2022). *4th stress test exercise for central counterparties*.

European Systemic Risk Board. (2020). *Mitigating the procyclicality of margins and haircuts in derivatives markets and securities financing transactions*. European Systemic Risk Board, European System of Financial Supervision.

Ewald, C. O., Haugom, E., Lien, G., Song, P., & Stødal, S. (2022). Riding the Nordic German power-spread: The Einar Aas experiment. *The Energy Journal, 43*(5).

Faruqui, U., Huang, W., & Takáts, E. (2018). Clearing risks in OTC derivatives markets: The CCP-bank nexus. *BIS Quarterly Review*, December.

Financial Stability Board (FSB). (2020). *Holistic review of the march market turmoil*. Financial Stability Board.

Garvin, N. (2012). Central counterparty interoperability. *RBA Bulletin,* June, 59–68.

Glaser, F., & Panz, S. (2016). *(Pro?)-cyclicality of collateral haircuts and systemic illiquidity*. European systemic risk board working paper series no. 27.

Gregory, J. (2014). *Central counterparties: mandatory central clearing and initial margin requirements for OTC derivatives*. Wiley.

Huang, W., & Takáts, E. (2020). *The CCP-bank nexus in the time of Covid-19*. Bank for International Settlements Bulletin No. 13.

Hull, J. (2012). CCPs: Their risks, and how they can be reduced. *The Journal of Derivatives, 20*(1), 26–29.

International Swaps and Derivatives Association (ISDA). (2021). *COVID-19 and CCP risk management frameworks*, January 2021, 1–12.

King, T. B., Nesmith, T. D., Paulson, A. L., & Prono, T. (2020). *Central clearing and systemic liquidity risk*, Finance and Economics Discussion Series, 2020-009.

Kroszner, R. (2006). Central counterparty clearing: History, innovation, and regulation. *Economic Perspectives, 30*(4).

Mallaby, S. (2016). *The man who knew: The life and times of Alan Greenspan*. Bloomsbury Publishing.

McCrank, J. (2022). *Commodities market volatility sparks spillover concerns*. Reuters. Available at: https://www.reuters.com/article/ukraine-crisis-ice-clearinghouses-idCNL2N2VB2FM

Monnet, C. (2010). *Let's make it clear: how central counterparties save(d) the day*. B usiness Review.

Moser, J. T. (1994). Origins of the modern exchange clearinghouse: A history of early clearing and settlement methods at futures exchanges. *Federal Reserve Bank of Chicago Working Paper Series* No. 94-3.

Mourselas, C. (2022). *Energy firms call for central bank support to cover margin spikes*. Risk.net. Available at: https://www.risk.net/risk-management/7938691/energy-firms-call-for-central-bank-support-to-cover-margin-spikes

Murphy, D., & Vause, N. (2021). *A CBA of APC: Analysing approaches to procyclicality reduction in CCP initial margin models*. Bank of England Staff Working Paper No. 950.

Murphy, D., Vasios, M., & Vause, N. (2014). *An investigation into the procyclicality of risk-based initial margin models*. Bank of England Financial Stability Paper No. 29.

Norman, P. (2011). *The risk controllers: central counterparty clearing in globalised financial markets*. Wiley.

Norman, B., Shaw, R., & Speight, G. (2011). *The history of interbank settlement arrangements: Exploring central banks' role in the payment system*. Bank of England Working Paper No. 412.

Nyborg, K. G. (2017). *Collateral frameworks: The open secret of central banks*. Cambridge University Press.

Priem, R. (2018). CCP recovery and resolution: Preventing a financial catastrophe. *Journal of Financial Regulation and Compliance, 26*(3), 351–364.

Ruffini, I., & Steigerwald, R. S. (2014). OTC derivatives—A primer on market infrastructure and regulatory policy. *Economic Perspectives, 38*(3), 80–100.

Thomadakis, A., & Lannoo, K. (2021). *Setting EU CCP policy–much more than meets the eye*. European Capital Markets Institute and Centre for European Policy Studies.

Wendt, F., & Shabsigh, G. (2015). *Central counterparties: Addressing their too important to fail nature*. International Monetary Fund Working Paper No. 021.

7 FX Operations and CLS

7.1 Introduction

The continued importance of **US Dollar is epitomised through its role as the global reserve currency**. The International Monetary Fund (2020) estimate that with respect to the US Dollar, (1) half of global trade is invoiced in it; (2) two-thirds of central bank foreign reserves are denominated in US Dollars; and (3) 45% of FX trading involves the US Dollar (see also Gopinath, 2017; Gopinath et al., 2020). This is despite the internationalisation of the Chinese Renminbi and the introduction of the euro (International Monetary Fund, 2020), and recent reported tendencies of nations like China, Russia, India and Brazil to de-dollarize their trade and FX reserves.

Aside from drawing down existing stocks of US Dollars within nostro accounts at correspondent banks (as shown in Chap. 5), there exist several other avenues through which banks are able to raise US Dollars so as finance cross-border flows. Certainly, the US Dollar funding network is extensive, consisting of a diverse set of intermediaries and financial instruments.

US Dollar funding is also geographically dispersed. For instance, many non-US banks raise US Dollars through a reliance on branches and subsidiaries (which act as correspondents to their headquarters) located in the United States. McCauley et al. (2019) estimate that of the $27 trillion in cross-border claims (as of Q4 2016), approximately $9 trillion constituted intragroup claims. But since the Global Financial Crisis, the use of such methods for European banks has declined. In contrast, non-European banks have increased their dependence on branches and subsidiaries (Aldasoro & Ehlers, 2018).

Although US Dollar denominated cross-border interbank claims (excluding inter-office loans) are sizeable ($1.8 trillion), FX trading (e.g. spot, outright forward, swaps) plays a dominant role in US Dollar funding. According to the Bank of International Settlements (2019a), daily trading in FX markets during 2019 was approximately $6.6 trillion, with **spot** transactions equating to $2 trillion and

U. Bindseil, G. Pantelopoulos, *Introduction to Payments and Financial Market Infrastructures*, Springer Texts in Business and Economics,
https://doi.org/10.1007/978-3-031-39520-8_7

outright forward trades equalling $1 trillion. Yet by far the largest instrument in FX turnover were **FX swaps (spot + forward)**, which were valued at $3.2 trillion. Indeed whilst the share of spot trades continued to fall in comparison with other instruments, FX swaps continued to gain market share. In parallel, the dominance of the US Dollar has continued, as 88% of all trades involve the US Dollar (Bank of International Settlements, 2019b). On the basis of daily trading, total gross obligations in 2019 totalled $18.8 trillion: being $2 trillion in spot transactions, $4 trillion in forwards and $12.8 trillion in FX swaps.

FX spot trade settlement is not instantaneous, but typically on T + 2, i.e. 2 days after the trade. **FX spot trade** settlement occurs over two legs. In the first leg, one bank grants the other domestic currency, with the other bank reciprocating in the second leg (Schaller, 2007). In comparison, settlement of a **FX swap** consists of four legs, as there exist two legs for both the spot and forward legs.

As the operating hours of payment and settlement systems in many cases do not immediately overlap due to time-zone differentials, counterparties had accepted for a long time (and still do in some currencies) credit risk in FX settlement, i.e. that the two legs occur without a link, and that if one party delivers and the other does not and defaults, then the first party may lose the entire notional value of the FX transaction (Baba et al., 2008). Therefore, ideally, the settlement of the two legs is linked through a process that achieves "payment versus payment" (PvP) which is defined as a settlement mechanism that ensures that the final transfer of a payment in one currency occurs if and only if the final transfer of a payment in another currency (or currencies) takes place. Owing to the extensive volumes of FX trading, non PvP settlement risks have the potential to create large systemic risks on the international financial system as a whole (Kos & Levich, 2016).

7.2 Herstatt Risk and the Origins of CLS

The risks associated with the non-settlement of a FX trade is often denoted as Herstatt risk Founded in 1956, on 26 June 1974 Herstatt Bank failed to settle its leg of several FX swaps, which resulted in its bankruptcy (DeRosa, 2013, 172). With German regulators revoking its ability to operate at 15:30 CET, Herstatt Bank's New York correspondent (Chase Manhattan Bank) immediately suspended all payments in US Dollars owed by Herstatt. The result was that counterparties incurred significant losses, as although having paid-in in Deutsche Marks, they did not receive US Dollars in exchange (BdF, 2018, 131; see also Swiss National Bank, 2009).

Herstatt risk can not only be associated with settlement failure, but also in the event where counterparties are simply unwilling to settle. For example, Kahn and Roberds (2001) comment that during the 1990 collapse of Drexel Burnham Lambert, one of its London based subsidiaries (Drexel Burnham Lambert Trading—DBLT) had been very active in the FX swap market. On the one hand (despite its fundamental solvency), counterparties became less willing to honour their commitments to

DBLT, as it was feared that DBLT would default on its obligations. On the other hand, DBLT also became reluctant to settle any swaps.

In the shadow of Herstatt Bank's failure—and in conjunction with other settlement failures involving FX trades (see DeRosa, 2013, 173)—the central banks of the G10 commissioned several studies in a bid to manage settlement risks (e.g. 1990 Lamfalussy report; 1993 Noel report) (BdF, 2018, 131). The 1996 Allsopp report established that settlement risks in FX trading were underestimated and not well managed. In view of this, three measures were recommended:

- (1) Action by individual banks to improve both the measurement and management of settlement risk;
- (2) Action by industry groups and service providers to devise and implement risk-reducing multi-currency services;
- (3) Initiatives by central banks to support such efforts through improving the services of each respective RTGS system. Although netting mechanisms that reduced exposure and settlement risks already existed, residual exposures remained following the process of netting. As a consequence, **PvP** was proposed as a remedy, as any legs of a FX trade would be settled simultaneously. This, in turn, led to the creation of **Continuous Linked Settlement (CLS)** (CPSS, 1996).

Owing to the complexities, the practical implementation of FX trades being settled on a PvP basis via CLS took some time. Located in New York, CLS is operated by CLS Bank, which acts as the settlement agent to direct settlement members for the purposes of completing several types of FX trades (BdF, 2018, 134). Strictly speaking, although CLS Bank is supervised by the Federal Reserve in conjunction with several other central banks, it is owned by a holding company, which in turn is owned by 75 other financial institutions (CPSS, 2008; ECB, 2010, 183).

Although in the majority of cases there is no direct legal compulsion for counterparties to settle FX trades through CLS, it has nevertheless proven to be successful (Kahn et al., 2014). In accordance with CLS Group (2021), more than 70 institutions are direct settlement members, with a further 25,000 banks utilising CLS via intermediaries. On any given day, more than $6 trillion of FX trades are settled through CLS in 18 currencies.

7.3 CLS Operational Framework

CLS operates through direct settlement members being equipped with a multicurrency account at CLS Bank, with the multicurrency account further subdivided into multiple accounts—one account for each currency to be settled through CLS. Moreover, CLS Bank holds accounts with the central banks that issue the currencies being traded (CPSS, 2008; BdF, 2018, 134).

At the start of a typical day, direct settlement members will begin the settlement cycle with a zero balance across all their accounts vis-à-vis CLS Bank. Hence at the end of the settlement cycle, CLS Bank holds no assets or liabilities with settlement members nor with any central banks (Miller & Northcott, 2002). Through a process known as funding, settlement members load their account with CLS Bank through their respective central banks, and can also reduce their funds with CLS Bank throughout the day by defunding. Both funding and defunding ensures that direct settlement members are equipped with sufficient stocks of currency in their accounts prior to settlement. Yet as CLS calculates a net position per currency for each member, the total amount of funding is profoundly reduced (ECB, 2010, 185).

In other words, although members send their payment instructions to CLS on a gross basis, post-trade claims and liabilities as a result of FX trades being agreed upon are **centrally cleared and then netted on a multilateral basis**. Through clearing and multilateral netting, CLS calculates a single net position in each currency for every direct settlement member. For instance, in the event that CLS determines that a member posts a **net negative currency position, they are required to pay-in** (subject to a predetermined schedule) and thus incur a liability vis-à-vis CLS Bank. On the flipside, should CLS calculate that a member posts a **net positive currency position**, the member will post a claim vis-a-vis CLS Bank and the latter will complete a **pay-out to the member (broken arrows)** (BdF, 2018, 134).

CLS applies a rigorous risk management scheme through the application of three main risk control measures. **First**, as CLS Bank cannot extend credit lines to settlement member, a participant's overall balance across **all of its currency subaccounts must always be positive**, despite the fact that individual currency subaccounts will incur a positive or negative balance at various stages (ECB, 2010, 185). To protect itself from any exchange rate volatility, CLS Bank calculates currency account balances in a base currency (typically US Dollars), and applies a valuation haircut to these balances to protect itself in the event of sudden exchange rate fluctuations (Miller & Northcott, 2002). It is important to emphasise **that haircuts increase "short" positions (i.e. increasing the amount that a member must pay-in), whilst at same time decrease "long" positions (i.e. thereby decreasing the amount of CLS must pay-out).** **Second**, CLS Bank sets a threshold regarding the negative position a settlement member can incur within **one individual currency subaccount**, otherwise known as the **Short Position Limit (SPL)**, which is identical for every settlement in a given currency (Miller & Northcott, 2002; BdF, 2018, 136). **Third**, CLS Bank also sets limits on the negative positions that a participant can accumulate **in aggregate**, known as the **Aggregate Short Position Limit (ASPL)**. Settlement members that are deemed to be higher risk incur more stringent limits on the degree to which currency accounts can incur a negative balance. Thus, the settlement of a trade only takes place on the proviso that all parties are able to comply with all CLS's risk management protocols. Assuming that all risk controls are fulfilled, settlement then occurs on a PvP basis (CPSS, 2008).

Should a direct settlement member miss a pay-in deadline, CLS is equipped with several options to ensure that the other settlement member receives its pay-out. As a first port of call, CLS suspends pay-outs to any settlement member that has failed to pay-in until its obligations are met. Next, CLS issues a pay-in call, requesting that the member top-up its account. Should the member fail to respond, through pre-arranged agreements CLS will contact other financial institutions as a means to obtain the necessary liquidity to complete a FX trade. If this were to fail, CLS can carry the amount remaining to be settled forward to the next business day (Miller & Northcott, 2002; BdF, 2018, 138).

7.4 FX Trade: non-PvP Settlement Outside CLS

In this section we illustrate **non-PvP FX settlement** by assuming a certain FX trade situation, which we will then replicate again in the subsequent section under the assumption that settlement occurs via CLS and is therefore PvP.

We take a currency pair which is not settled in CLS, namely USD-Turkish Lira (as the latter is not in CLS). We assume that Denizbank (located in Istanbul) uses Citibank in the US as its correspondent bank (i.e. Denizbank has no branch or subsidiary in the US) for making US Dollar payments on behalf of its customers.

- **T = 0:** Suppose that a **Turkish industrial firm**, who has its deposit account with Denizbank, needs to import an expensive machine from the US. The firm gives prior notice to the Turkish bank that at T + 4 it will have to make a payment to a US based supplier which has an account with the US middle sized bank Pacific Western Bank. The payment has a value of "a" that is denominated in US Dollars.
- **T = 0:** Denizbank needs to purchase USD for that in advance, and in any case wants to replenish its USD position on its correspondent banking account with Citibank. As it would like to receive the best possible FX rate in the market, it goes to a trading platform in which it purchases immediately "b" US Dollars (where $b > a$) against "βb" Turkish Lira, for settlement in T + 2 (β is the amount of Turkish Liras required to purchase 1 US Dollar). Its trading counterparty is Deutsche Bank NY. The settlement instructions clarify that on T + 2, the USD should be settled via a transfer order from Deutsche Bank NY to Citibank for the benefit of Denizbank. Deutsche Bank NY also clarifies that the Lira leg should be settled with the Deutsche Bank subsidiary in Istanbul (i.e. Deutsche Bank is assumed to not require a separate correspondent bank as it itself has established a branch in Istanbul). The FX trade means that before settlement, there is now a claim of Denizbank towards Deutsche Bank NY as the latter will provide USD, and Deutsche Bank NY has a claim against Denizbank as the latter will provide Turkish Lira—the creation of these claims is shown as flow **b1** in the financial accounts (when denominated in USD, or conversely in Turkish Lira, as flow **βb1**).
- **T + 2:** The settlement of **b** and of **βb** occur, which is shown as flow **b2** and **b3** in the accounts and can be explained in the following way. Sometime on the same day (presumably a few hours earlier than the US leg, because of the time zone difference) Denizbank transfers **βb2** through the Turkish RTGS system to Deutsche Bank's subsidiary in Turkey **(b2)**. A few hours later, Deutsche Bank NY then transfers the USD leg via Fedwire to Citibank **(b3)**. Citibank interprets the information received through messaging correctly and notifies Denizbank on

T + 2 that the money from Deutsche Bank NY has arrived and that it understood that the money was sent for the benefit of the vostro account of Denizbank. What happens on this day from the perspective of Denizbank is that an IOU type of claim towards Deutsche Bank to deliver on a dollar payment is replaced by a position in a vostro account of Citibank—in some sense also an IOU. Nevertheless, this can be considered "settlement" for two reasons. First, **Denizbank selected Citibank out of all alternatives as a correspondent bank, presumably because of its high rating, reputation**, and maybe its perceived too-big-to fail status. Also, Deutsche Bank may have a good rating, but it was not selected as a FX counterparty because of its good rating, but because of the attractive FX rate it quoted, and the bank providing the best quote could also have had a significantly lower rating. Second, **Denizbank uses its correspondent account with Citibank for a multitude of cash inflows and outflows**, and does its centralised USD liquidity management there. In so far, the inflow resulting from the settlement of the FX trade with Deutsche Bank is not structurally increasing its exposure, but presumably remains exposure neutral as it is there to match outflows that Denizbank foresees for various reasons (including the need to make a payment to the US exporter as ordered by its Turkish client).
- **T + 3:** Denizbank instructs Citibank to transfer "a" US Dollars to Pacific Western Bank for the benefit of the American exporter, such that the money will be debited to the latter's deposit account with that bank on T + 4. This last operation is no longer part of the FX ettlement, but is just a usage of the funds obtained through the FX trade (Table 7.1).

With the FX spot trade settled without a dedicated third-party settlement agent, there is limited scope for reducing post-trade claims and liabilities through netting. Furthermore, there is no mechanism to ensure that the first leg is completed on the proviso that the second leg will be completed and vice versa (Lindley, 2008). In other words, since the spot trade is undertaken on a **non PvP basis**, both banks are exposed to settlement risk. Also, the failure of one bank could lead to a domino effect on banks which were counterparties to other transactions, and hence, there is an increased likelihood of systemic risks (DeRosa, 2013, 182).

7.5 FX Trade: PvP Settlement Through CLS

To showcase **PvP FX settlement**, we keep the example above unchanged, but for the fact that we replace Turkey by Mexico, as the Peso is in CLS and therefore so is the currency pair USD-Mexican Peso. Consider the following steps:

- **T = 0:** Banco Azteca (i.e. the bank of the importer) and Deutsche Bank NY enter into a FX spot trade in the amount of "b" (where b > a). Banco Azteca is relatively small and is not a CLS settlement member. Both Deutsche Bank and Citibank are CLS settlement members (see "Master List of Members of CLS Bank International as of December 7, 2020", as provided on the CLS website).

Table 7.1 FX Spot trade outside of CLS.

Turkey - accounts in Turkish Lira							
Denizbank							
Deposits at CB Turkey	X	-βb2		Deposits of importer	X		-βa
USD Nostro with Citibank	X	+βb3	-βa	Liability to Deutsche NY		+βb1 -βb2	
USD claim on Deutsche NY		+βb1 -βb3		Equity	X		
Deutsche Bank subsidiary in Turkey							
Deposits at CB Turkey	X	+βb2		Intra-DB group liability	X	+βb2	
				Equity	X		
Central Bank of Turkey							
Other assets	X			Deposits Deutsche Bank	X	+βb2	
				Deposits of Denizbank	X	-βb2	
				Equity	X		
United States – accounts in US Dollars							
Citibank							
Deposits at Fed	X	+b3	-a	Vostro Denizbank	X	+b3	-a
				Equity	X		
Deutsche Bank NY							
Deposits at Fed	X	−b3		Liability to Denizbank		+b1 −b3	
Lira Claim on Denizbank	X	+b1 −b3		Equity	X		
Intra-DB group claim	X	+b3					
Pacific Western Bank							
Deposits at central bank	X		+a	Deposits of Exporter	X		+a
				Equity	X		
US central bank - Fed							
Other assets	X			Deposits Citibank	X	+b3	-a
				Deposits Deutsche NY	X	−b3	
				Deposits Pacific Western	X		+a
				Equity	X		

Moreover, Deutsche Bank has subsidiaries in Mexico (Deutsche Bank Mexico, S. A.) and in New York, and Citibank, the USD correspondent bank of Banco Azteca and its FX settlement agent for USD-MXN, has subsidiaries on both sides as well (Citi operates in Mexico as Citibanamex S.A.).

- **T = 0:** The settlement instructions and related general contractual agreements specify that on T + 2, the FX spot trade will be settled through CLS and that on T + 1, Banco Azteca will shift central bank money via the Mexican RTGS system to the Mexican subsidiary of Citibank in Mexico (assuming that it would use Citibank also for that on the Mexican Peso side). Also, Citibank NY—as the US correspondent bank of Banco Azteca—will credit on T + 2 the vostro account of Banco Azteca, once the settlement of both legs of the FX trade have taken place via CLS. After entering into the trade, Banco Azteca has an IOU-like USD claim vis-à-vis Deutsche Bank NY, which is represented in the accounts as "βb1". Similarly, Deutsche Bank NY has an IOU-like MXN claim on Banco Azteca, which is shown in the accounts as "b1".
- **T = 1:** Banco Azteca shifts central bank money via the Mexican RTGS system to Citibank's subsidiary in Mexico, and the former now has an IOU-like claim on the latter **(b2).**

- **T = 2:** As the time zones of Mexico City and New York (and hence the operating hours of both RTGS systems as operated by the Fed and the Banco del Mexico) are largely similar, the transfer of funds into the CLS accounts take place more or less at a similar time in the morning of T + 2 (CLS defines exactly the deadlines when the money must have been received by CLS). Thus, Deutsche Bank NY transfers USD from its RTGS account at the Fed to CLS Bank's account with the Fed, and Citibank's subsidiary in Mexico transfers Mexican Peso into CLS Bank's account with the Banco del Mexico **(b3)**. Note that alternatively, the steps associated with b2 and b3 could also be merged in the sense that Banco Azteca could directly transfer the MXN amount from its RTGS account to the RTGS account of CLS for the benefit of Citibank Mexico's account with CLS, even without being itself a settlement member. The RTGS transfer instructions would have to contain the necessary information so that CLS can assign these MXN funds received to the right settlement member, Citibank. We do not show this case in the accounts. Further, here we are assuming that in effect both Deutsche Bank and Citibank post a net negative position vis-à-vis CLS Bank, but at the same time post and a net positive position following all other payment instructions being cleared and netted.
- **T = 2:** At this point, CLS Bank recognises that both settlement members have paid-in the relevant amounts in both currencies. It can now swap the currencies on a PvP basis, by simultaneously debiting Deutsche Bank NY in USD and by crediting Citibank NY in USD, and at the same time by debiting Citibank Mexico in Mexican Peso and by crediting Deutsche Bank Mexico in Peso. This also results in both the Deutsche Bank group and the Citibank group posting intra-group claims and liabilities **(b4)**.
- **T = 2:** CLS Bank then shifts central bank money via the respective local RTGS systems back to the settlement member banks to bring its own account with the two central banks back to zero. That is to say, CLS Bank transfers USD to Citibank NY, and Mexican Pesos to Deutsche Bank Mexico **(b5)**. CLS Bank's deposits in each central bank now fall back to zero. The initial claims and liabilities between Banco Azteca and Deutsche Bank NY now disappear—and the FX spot trade is settled—as Citibank NY credits the vostro account of Banco Azteca, which also eliminates the claim of Banco Azteca vis-à-vis Citibank's subsidiary in Mexico (and also Citibank NY's intra-group liability to Citibank Mexico) **(b6).**
- **T = 3:** Banco Azteca instructs Citibank NY to transfer US Dollars to Pacific Western Bank for the benefit of the American exporter (this and the next step are outside the FX trade and its settlement).
- **T = 4:** The deposit account of the exporter is credited in the amount of "a" (Table 7.2).

By completing the FX spot trade through CLS Bank, **there is never a point where one leg is settled but the other is not**. Hence, participants are never exposed to any settlement risk (Kahn et al., 2014). But whilst heavily reduced, CLS does not completely eliminate liquidity risk (not per conceptual construction but out of

Table 7.2 FX Spot trade settlement with CLS.

Assets	Initial	Flows	Liabilities	Initial	Flows
Mexico - accounts in Mexican Pesos (MXN)					
Banco Azteca					
Deposits at CB Mexico	X	-βb2	Deposits of importer	X	-βa
USD Nostro Citibank NY	X	+βb6 -βa	Equity	X	
USD claim on DB NY		+βb1 -βb6	Liability to DB NY		+βb1 -βb6
Claim on Citibank Mex		+βb2 -βb6			
Citibank Mexico					
Deposits with CB Mexico	X	+βb2 -βb3	Liability to Banco Azteca		+βb2 -βb6
Account with CLS		+βb3 -βb4	liability		
Intra-Citi group claim		+βb4 -βb6	Equity	X	
Deutsche Bank Mexico					
Deposit with CB Mexico	X	+βb5	Intra-DB group liability		+βb4
Account with CLS		+βb4 -βb5	Equity	X	
CLS Bank Mexico					
Deposits with CB Mexico		+βb3 -βb5	Account of Citibank Mex		+βb3 -βb4
			Account of DB Mex		+βb4 -βb5
Central Bank of Mexico					
Other assets	X		Deposits of Banco Azteca	X	-βb2
			Deposits DB Mex	X	+βb5
			Deposits Citibank Mex	X	+βb2 -βb3
			Deposits CLS Bank		+βb3 -βb5
			Equity	X	
United States – accounts in US Dollars					
Citibank NY					
Deposits at Fed	X	+b5 -a	Vostro Banco Azteca	X	+b6 -a
Intra-Citi group claim			Intra-Citi group liability		+b4 -b6
Account with CLS		+b4 -b5	Equity		
Deutsche Bank NY					
Deposit with Fed	X	-b3	Liability to Banco Azteca		+b1 -b6
MXN claim on B. Azteca		+b1 -b6	Equity	X	
Account with CLS		+b3 -b4			
Intra-DB group claim		+b4			
Pacific Western Bank					
Deposits at Fed	X	+a	Deposits of Exporter	X	+a
			Equity	X	
CLS Bank United States					
Deposits with Fed		+b3 -b5	Account of DB NY		+b3 -b4
			Account of Citibank NY		+b4 -b5
US central bank - Fed					
Other assets	X		Deposits Citibank NY	X	+b5 -a
			Deposits DB NY	X	-b3
			Deposits Pacific Western	X	+a
			Deposits CLS Bank		+b3 -b5
			Equity	X	

pragmatism to not consume excessive amounts of liquidity, i.e. as a result of a deliberate choice made). For example, as final pay-ins are calculated on a multilateral net basis, the failure of one member to pay in may cause delays in the settlement of other trades and will thereby result in the net pay-in schedule being recalculated at very short notice. Thus, a member which was originally being paid-out may have to pay-in.

Without a real loss of generality, the above flows can be shown in net terms (we ignore CLS in the accounts below, as CLS only has a "temporary" balance sheet). We include two flows: the first being "b"—which is equal to the FX spot trade—and "a", which is equal to the payment that the importer makes for the machine from the United States (where b > a) (Table 7.3).

Table 7.3 FX Spot trade settlement with CLS—net terms

Mexico - accounts in Mexican Pesos (MXN)			
Banco Azteca			
Deposits at CB Mexico	X **-βb**	Deposits of importer	X -βa
USD Nostro Citibank NY	X **+βb** -βa	Equity	X
Deutsche Bank Mexico			
Deposit with CB Mexico	X **+βb**	Intra-DB group liability	**+βb**
		Equity	X
Central Bank of Mexico			
Other assets	X	Deposits of Banco Azteca	X **-βb**
		Deposits DB Mex	X **+βb**
		Deposits Citibank Mex	X
		Equity	X
United States – accounts in US Dollars			
Citibank NY			
Deposits at Fed	X **+b** -a	Vostro Banco Azteca	X **+b** -a
		Intra-Citi group liability	X
		Equity	
Deutsche Bank NY			
Deposit with Fed	X **-b**	Equity	X
Intra-DB group claim	**+b**		
Pacific Western Bank			
Deposits at Fed	X +a	Deposits of Exporter	X +a
		Equity	X
US central bank - Fed			
Other assets	X	Deposits Citibank NY	X **+b** -a
		Deposits DB NY	X **-b**
		Deposits Pacific Western	X +a
		Equity	X

Despite the widespread uptake of CLS, settlement risk has not been completely eradicated within the FX market. Indeed in recent years, non PvP settlement has actually increased, mainly owing to the growth of currencies being traded which are not eligible for CLS (Schrimpf & Sushko, 2019). This is despite the introduction of CLSnet, which allows for the bilateral netting of FX trades for around 120 currencies (CLS Group, 2022) and which allows to some extent to reduce settlement values also in non-DvP currencies.

References

Aldasoro, I., & Ehlers, T. (2018). The geography of dollar funding of non-US banks. *BIS Quarterly Review December*.

Baba, N., Packer, F., & Nagano, T. (2008). The spillover of money market turbulence to FX swap and cross-currency swap markets. *BIS Quarterly Review*, March.

Bank of International Settlements. (2019a). *Triennial Central Bank Survey, Foreign Exchange and Over-the-counter (OTC) Derivatives Markets in 2019*. Monetary and Economic Department.

Bank of International Settlements. (2019b). *Triennial Central Bank Survey, Foreign Exchange Turnover in April 2019*. Monetary and Economic Department.

BdF. (2018). *Payments and market infrastructure in the digital age*. BdF Publication.

Continuous Linked Settlement Bank International (CLS Group). (2021). *CLS in numbers*. Available at: https://www.cls-group.com/

Continuous Linked Settlement Bank International (CLS Group). (2022). *CLSnet*. Available at: https://www.cls-group.com/products/processing/clsnet/#:~:text=CLSNet%20is%20a%20standardized%2C%20automated,trade%20matching%20and%20netting%20processes

CPSS. (1996). Settlement risk in foreign exchange transactions. Report prepared by the *Committee on Payment and Settlement Systems of the Central Banks of the Group of Ten Countries*, Bank of International Settlements, Basle.
CPSS. (2008). *Progress in reducing foreign exchange settlement risk.* Bank of International Settlements.
DeRosa, D. F. (2013). *Foreign exchange operations: Master trading agreements, settlement, and collateral.* Wiley.
ECB. (2010). *The payment system, payments, securities and derivatives, and the role of the Eurosystem.*
Gopinath, G. (2017). Rethinking macroeconomic policy: International economy issues. In *Rethinking Macroeconomic Policy Conference*, Peterson Institute for International Economics, October.
Gopinath, G., Boz, E., Casas, C., Díez, F. J., Gourinchas, P. O., & Plagborg-Møller, M. (2020). Dominant currency paradigm. *American Economic Review, 110*(3), 677–719.
International Monetary Fund. (2020). *Reserve currencies in an evolving international monetary system.* International Monetary Fund Strategy, Policy and Review Department, No. 20/02, Washington, DC.
Kahn, C. M., & Roberds, W. (2001). *The CLS bank: A solution to the risks of international payments settlement?* Federal Reserve Bank of Atlanta Working Paper No. 2000-15a.
Kahn, C., Quinn, S., & Roberds, W. (2014). Central banks and payment systems: The evolving trade-off between cost and risk. In *Norges Bank conference on the uses of central banks: Lessons from history.*
Kos, D., & Levich, R. M. (2016). *Settlement risk in the global FX market: How much remains?* Available at SSRN 2827530.
Lindley, R. (2008). Reducing foreign exchange settlement risk. *BIS Quarterly Review,* September.
McCauley, R. N., Bénétrix, A. S., McGuire, P. M., & von Peter, G. (2019). Financial deglobalisation in banking? *Journal of International Money and Finance, 94*, 116–131.
Miller, P., & Northcott, C. A. (2002). CLS Bank: Managing foreign exchange settlement risk. *Bank of Canada Review, 2002*(Autumn), 13–25.
Schaller, A. (2007). *Continuous linked settlement: History and implications* (Doctoral dissertation, University of Zurich).
Schrimpf, A., & Sushko, V. (2019). FX trade execution: complex and highly fragmented. *BIS Quarterly Review,* December.
Swiss National Bank. (2009). *The Continuous Linked Settlement foreign exchange settlement system (CLS).* Basle.

Central Securities Depositories

8

8.1 Introduction

Central securities depositories (CSDs) provide securities accounts in addition to centralised asset and safekeeping services, as they ensure that any securities are not created or destroyed (either by accident or by fraudulent means). Typically, **a CSD will also serve as a securities settlement system (SSS)** (CPSS-IOSCO, 2012, 72–73; Bech et al., 2020c). Through clearing and settlement, CSDs manage the post-trade aspect of any securities transaction following a trade being agreed upon. CSDs are a key FMI, particularly since trading in both domestic and cross-border securities markets has increased considerably during recent decades (Van Cayseele & Wuyts, 2007).

One of the motivations behind the introduction of CSDs was to **immobilise** the movement of paper when securities ownership changed hands. Through technological advancements, securities were then **dematerialised**, and began to exist only in electronic form at the CSD (Bech et al., 2020b). Given the obvious advances for efficiency, the introduction of immobilisation and/or dematerialisation has received broad support by participants (Chan et al., 2007). The first instance of immobalisation occurred in the nineteenth century in Berlin, through the *Kassenverein* (Mueller, 1910, 232; see also Moles and Terry, 1997, 159). The second occurrence of immoblisation occurred in 1942 in France, with the majority of other CSDs in Europe founded during the 1960s. In the United States, a paperwork crisis served as a catalyst to accelerate the introduction of CSDs, with the Depository Trust Company formed in 1973 (Chan et al., 2007). Whilst **domestic securities settlement** can in principle occur across the books of a single CSD, any **cross-border trade in securities** can take place via one or several intermediaries, namely through **large custodian banks** and **International CSDs (ICSDs)** (CPSS, 1995; Comotto, 2011).

U. Bindseil, G. Pantelopoulos, *Introduction to Payments and Financial Market Infrastructures*, Springer Texts in Business and Economics,
https://doi.org/10.1007/978-3-031-39520-8_8

8.2 Key Activities of CSDs

CSDs maintain securities accounts mostly on behalf of financial intermediaries, who in turn keep these securities on their books for their clients (i.e. investors). This is known as the **indirect holding model**. In some instances, intermediaries may not even hold a securities account with the CSD, and must rely on **custodian banks**, which are equipped with an account at the CSD. The underlying characteristic of such an arrangement is that there may be **several degrees of separation** between the CSD and investors, as there is no theoretical limit to the number of layers in the chain of ownership (e.g. Investor 1 has a securities account with Bank 1, which in turn has a securities account with Bank 2, that in turn has an account with Bank 3—in this sequence, only Bank 3 has a securities account at the CSD). The existence of multiple intermediaries between the CSD and end-investors is in contrast to the **direct holding model**, in which the securities of investors are held directly at the CSD (i.e. the CSD maintains accounts in the name of end-investors) (Bech et al., 2020d).

Irrespective of whether the indirect or direct holding model is adopted, CSDs provide a **notary service** through initially verifying and recording any newly created securities by liaising with securities issuers. In doing so, each instrument is allocated an **ISIN code**. CSDs are also fundamental to ensuring **successful securities settlement**. After a trade is struck between two parties, the **confirmation process** begins, where the price, quantity, and identity of securities is confirmed. In recent years, confirmation has become more streamlined due to straight-through processing for the majority of domestic trades. On the other hand, manual procedures are still adhered to for some cross-border securities trades (BdF, 2018, 215). The **final settlement date** is also determined during the confirmation process. In the late 1980s, it was recommended by the G30 (1988) that the settlement cycle be shortened to be no later than T + 3. Consequently, settlement is now one day shorter (i.e. T + 2) in a large number of economies (e.g. EU member nations). In the United States, it is envisaged that settlement cycles will be further reduced to T + 1 by 2024 (Thomadakis, 2022).

Following the confirmation process, **matching** begins through intermediaries conferring with the CSD that the confirmation process has been completed successfully. This is achieved through a comparison of "matching criteria" (e.g. the type of securities, what securities accounts and what cash accounts, settlement date). Once matching is complete, the instructions become irrevocable (BdF, 2018, 215–216).

The settlement of securities may be classified as follows according to the existence and nature of a counterbalancing flow:

- **Delivery versus payment (DvP):** securities settlement which ensures that delivery occurs on the proviso that payment occurs. This is key to safeguarding the minimization of counterparty credit risk. CPSS (1992) identify three models of DvP systems, whereby the first is to be considered standard and the most genuine form of DvP: **DvP model 1:** Gross simultaneous settlement of securities and funds on a one-by-one basis; **DvP model 2:** Gross settlement of securities transfers, with funds settled on a net basis at the end of the day; **DvP model 3:** Net simultaneous settlement of securities and funds.

- **Delivery versus delivery (DvD):** securities settlement which ensures that the delivery of a security occurs on the proviso that the other security is already transferred.
- **Free of payment (FoP):** securities settlement that is not linked to a corresponding payment leg, such as relating to the posting of collateral (margin) to a CCP.

The cash leg of any domestic securities settlement can take place in **commercial bank money**. In this case, intermediaries (i.e. banks) can hold cash accounts with other banks (i.e. custodians), who in turn hold cash accounts directly with the CSD. Alternatively, intermediaries may simply be directly linked to the CSD. There are also a number of models which enable the settlement of any cash leg to occur in **central bank money**. For instance, we can consider **two major variants** as outlined by the ECB (2004):

- In the **interfaced model**, intermediaries which are acting on behalf of their investor clients hold cash accounts directly at the central bank to facilitate the sale or purchase of securities. In turn, there is **no disconnect between RTGS cash accounts**, and **cash accounts used for settling the cash leg of any securities transaction**. On the other hand, securities accounts are held at the CSD, which are merely "subset" accounts of the central bank (if the CSD is controlled by the central bank). In this way, the interfaced model requires that the CSD and financial intermediaries interact across the books of the central bank.
- In the **integrated model**, the central bank essentially **outsources all processing activities to the CSD**, which operates on the accord of the central bank. Under such a scheme, **both settlement cash accounts and securities accounts of intermediaries are held at the CSD**, the former on the asset side, and the latter as liabilities. Also, **RTGS cash accounts and cash accounts used for securities settlement are segregated**. Whilst from a legal perspective the deposits of intermediaries held with the CSD are claims on the central bank, in reality from the point of view of end-users there is no real difference between the integrated and interfaced models.

Irrespective of whether settlement occurs in commercial bank or central bank money, many CSDs offer **intraday credit** (subject to adequate collateral being posted), which acts as a form of liquidity management tool to facilitate securities settlement. This requires that the CSD is equipped with a banking license. As a further liquidity management tool, some CSDs also provide an **auto-collateralisation** service when the payer is not equipped with sufficient funds in their cash account. As the name implies, such a service is automatic, and can be enacted either through a provision of credit via the same securities being purchased (known as "auto-collateralisation on-flow"), or through a stock of securities already held with the CSD ("auto-collateralisation on-stock") (ECB, 2022c).

8.3 The CSD and ICSD Landscape

The depth of trading in securities is concentrated in a handful of CSDs For instance, according to the European Central Securities Depositories Association's (2022) database, the largest CSDs in terms of the value of settlement instructions (DvP and FoP) processed across their books were Euroclear (Euroclear Bank—40.9%; Euroclear UK and Ireland—22.1%; Euroclear France—8.2%) and Clearstream (Clearstream Banking Luxembourg—16.7%; Clearstream Banking Germany—5.9%). Hence when taken together, Euroclear and Clearstream constitute around 94% of the total value of settlement instructions processed.

For a **domestic securities transaction**, arrangements can be quite straightforward. For example, it could be that the buyer and seller of a particular security hold deposit and securities accounts with a single bank, which in turn is equipped with deposit and securities accounts at the CSD. Settlement could then occur either in commercial bank money or central bank money. On the flipside, it is typical for **cross-border securities settlement** to require a larger number of intermediaries, namely **ICSDs** and **global custodian banks**.

Cross-border securities settlement services are nearly always executed in commercial bank money (ECB, 2014). As Comotto (2011) explains, without recourse to the cross-border securities settlement services offered by custodian banks and ICSDs, financial institutions would be forced to open branches or subsidiaries in every nation (or currency zone) where they participate, which is not realistic. If central banks were to provide multicurrency facilities, monetary authorities would be acting as a quasi-form of global settlement agent which would disrupt the desire for competition between public and private actors.

ICSDs first appeared in the late 1960s and early 1970s for the settlement of Eurobonds , which were introduced in part as a response to operational and regulatory inefficiences in domestic bond markets (Dickinson, 2015, 154). Eurobonds are instruments that are denominated in a different currency to that which is issued in the nation of the issuer (e.g. if a German corporation were to issue a debt instrument in US Dollars). The first Eurobond (denominated in US Dollars) was issued in 1958 by the Belgian Government in London. The Eurobond market then deepened significantly over time, in-part due to measures imposed by the US Government to circumvent constraints imposed by the Triffin (1960) dilemma (Emanuel, 1976; O'Malley, 2015, 21–44). As the vast majority of Eurobonds were issued and sold in Europe—but denominated in US Dollars—they were held physically in New York. Yet Dickinson (2015, 153) notes that by the late 1960s, the delivery of securities following trading on both the primary and secondary markets became subject to such a backlog that a large number of settlement failures occurred. Following this, some of the first ISCDs were established, being Euroclear and Clearstream, which were founded in 1968 and 1970, respectively (BdF, 2018, 210).

8.4 Domestic Securities Settlement

8.4.1 Domestic Securities Settlement in Commercial Bank Money

We can first show a **domestic DvP transaction** initiated by two investors who each have a deposit account at a different bank that takes place in **commercial bank money** as per the **indirect holding model** (i.e. investor's securities are held by intermediaries at the CSD). Suppose the two investors agree on the transaction at some trading venue, which passes on the instructions to "CSD Bank" and the bank of the payer and payee in preparation for settlement on T + 2. In this example, it is assumed that the amount of securities traded is in the amount of "a", and that both banks have cash and securities accounts at the CSD.

- On T + 2, Bank 1, the bank of Investor 1 (the payer—the buyer of securities), transfers commercial bank money in the amount of "a" to Bank 2, the bank of Investor 2 (the payee—the seller of securities). This completes the cash leg.
- On the proviso that funds have been successfully received (i.e. DvP)—the bank of Investor 2 sends instructions to CSD Bank which result in Investor 1 receiving a stock of securities. The securities leg has now been completed. Strictly speaking, CSD Bank could provide intra-day credit to Bank 1 to guarantee DvP (e.g. if Bank 1 were not to be equipped with a sufficient stock of deposits at CSD Bank), but here we ignore such a possibility (Table 8.1).

Table 8.1 DvP settlement in commercial bank money

Country X – in X currency			
Investor 1			
Deposits at Bank 1	X **-a**	Other liabilities	X
Securities with Bank 1	X **+a**	Equity	X
Bank 1			
Deposits at central bank	X	Other liabilities	X
Deposits at CSD Bank	X **-a**	Deposits	X **-a**
Securities at CSD Bank	X **+a**	Sec. account Investor 1	X **+a**
Other assets	X	Equity	X
CSD Bank			
Deposits at central bank	X	Other liabilities	X
Other assets	X	Securities account Bank 1	X **+a**
		Securities account Bank 2	X **-a**
		Deposits Bank 1	X **-a**
		Deposits Bank 2	X **+a**
		Equity	X
Bank 2			
Deposits at central bank	X	Other liabilities	X
Deposits at CSD Bank	X **+a**	Deposits	X **+a**
Securities at CSD Bank	X **-a**	Sec. account Investor 2	X **-a**
Other assets	X	Equity	X
Investor 2			
Deposits at Bank 2	X **+a**	Other liabilities	X
Securities with Bank 2	X **-a**	Equity	X

DvP is achieved, but in **commercial bank money**. The avoidance of any credit risks which DvP is supposed to achieve relies on the financial soundness and operational performance of CSD Bank. Thus, investors and banks should monitor the credit quality of CSD Bank. Still, it is a significant achievement that the investors and other banks **do not need to monitor their respective counterparties**, thanks to the DvP mechanism. The ability of CSD Bank to offer DvP would be reflected in its credit rating relative to other banks. For example, Fitch provides a "AA+" rating to Euroclear Bank (Belgium) and "AA" to Clearstream Bank SA (Luxembourg), while many other European banks have "A"or "BBB" ratings. For the users of the CSD, DvP in commercial bank money however requires the availability of deposits with the CSD, i.e. a separate pool of funds that needs to be financed. To enhance the efficiency of liquidity, i.e. allow for DvP with less net segregated funds for its clients, CSDs typically offer various collateral services in which the securities held by a client with the CSD are pledged to finance the funds that are used to settle new securities transactions in DvP. Moreover, **CSDs offer so-called "triparty collateral management services"** in which the triparty agent (the CSD) offers services to clients such that the clients can easily mobilise their securities holdings with the CSD as collateral to secure exposures across different products and instruments (e.g. repos, securities lending, central bank credit, secured loans and exposures arising from OTC transactions). As part of their daily operations, triparty agents provide services such as automatic selection and allocation of the collateral, valuation and substitution, optimisation of the composition of the triparty pool ("allocation cycles") and corporate actions processing. For example, Euroclear explains in its annual report for 2021 (p. 25):

> The Euroclear Collateral Highway supports the financial market's requirement for a neutral, interoperable utility to source, mobilise and segregate collateral. It provides a comprehensive solution for managing collateral, offering clients a complete view of exposures across the full spectrum of their asset classes and enabling them to benefit from collateral optimisation opportunities. In addition to more traditional collateral management activities (typically repos, securities lending, derivatives and access to central bank liquidity), Euroclear's range of collateral management solutions includes dedicated services for corporate treasurers, and a specialised equities collateral management service. By the end of 2021, the average daily collateralised outstanding on the Collateral Highway reached a record €1.9 trillion . . .

How would the above system of accounts look like if Investor 1 were to have their securities account with Bank 1, but the latter were to not be equipped with an account at CSD Bank? To be able to serve these clients, Bank 1 would presumably open a securities account with a large custody bank, Bank 3, who itself has an account with the CSD Bank (and with the majority of important CSDs worldwide). We show below only the accounts that change due to this additional intermediary, whereby we also assume that Bank 1 has a deposit account with Bank 3 for the purpose of Bank 3's securities intermediary services (alternatively, the related cash transfers could take place in the books of the central bank) (Table 8.2).

Table 8.2 DvP settlement in commercial bank money with a large custodian bank

Country X – in X currency			
Bank 1			
Deposits at central bank	X	Other liabilities	X
Deposits at Bank 3	X **-a**	Deposits	X **-a**
Securities at Bank 3	X **+a**	Sec. account Investor 1	X **+a**
Other assets	X	Equity	X
Bank 3 (large custodian)			
Deposits at central bank	X	Other liabilities	X
Deposits at CSD Bank	X **-a**	Sec. account Bank 1	X **+a**
Sec. account at CSD Bank	X **+a**	Deposits Bank 1	X **-a**
Other assets	X	Equity	X
CSD Bank			
Deposits at central bank	X	Other liabilities	X
Other assets	X	Sec. account Bank 2	X **-a**
		Sec. account Bank 3	X **+a**
		Deposits Bank 2	X **+a**
		Deposits Bank 3	X **-a**
		Equity	X

While the accounts of Investor 1, Investor 2 and Bank 2 remain unchanged, the cash and securities accounts of Bank 1 are now held with Bank 3. A longer custody chain of course implies potential risks relating to the additional intermediaries, in this case Bank 3. In theory, there is of course **no limit to the number of intermediate layers** (e.g. Bank 1 could rely on Bank 3, and Bank 3 could itself rely on Bank 4 which acts as a large custodian etc.). It is for such reasons that large custodian banks typically have a high credit quality. Large custody banks also play an important role in international securities settlement (see Sect. 8.5).

8.4.2 Non-DvP Securities Settlement in Central Bank Money

We can now demonstrate domestic securities settlement in **central bank money**. Suppose again that Investor 1 purchases a stock of securities from Investor 2 in the amount of "a". Since settlement is assumed to be non-DvP, settlement takes place in the following way:

- On T + 2, central bank money is transferred from the RTGS account of Bank 1 (the bank of Investor 1, the payer, or buyer of securities) to the RTGS account of Bank 2 **(a1)**.
- Without linking it to the payment confirmation (i.e. non-DvP), the CSD settles the securities transaction **(a2)**. Note that since settlement is non-DvP, there is strictly speaking no predetermined sequence between the above steps.
- Bank 2 credits the deposit account of its depositor (Investor 2, who sells the security) only after having settled the security leg. Banks do not want to take credit exposures to their clients, and therefore the assumption taken above that the

Table 8.3 Non-DvP settlement in central bank money

Country X – in X currency			
Investor 1			
Deposits at Bank 1	X -a1	Other liabilities	X
Claim on Bank 1	*+a1* *-a2*	Equity	X
Securities with Bank 1	X +a2		
Bank 1			
Deposits at central bank	X -a1	Other liabilities	X
Claim on Bank 2	*+a1–a2*	Deposits	X -a1
Securities at CSD	X +a2	*Liability to Investor 1*	*+a1* *-a2*
Other assets	X	Sec. account Investor 1	X +a2
		Equity	X
Central Bank			
Other assets	X	Other liabilities	X
		Bank 1 RTGS account	X –a1
		Bank 2 RTGS account	X +a1
		Banknotes	X
		Equity	X
CSD			
Other assets	X	Other liabilities	X
		Securities account Bank 1	X +a2
		Securities account Bank 2	X -a2
		Equity	X
Bank 2			
Deposits at central bank	X +a1	Other liabilities	X
Securities at CSD	X -a2	Deposits	X +a3
Other assets	X	*Liability to Bank 1*	*+a1–a2*
		Liability to Investor 2	*+a2* *-a3*
		Sec. account Investor 2	X -a2
		Equity	X
Investor 2			
Deposits at Bank 2	X +a3	Other liabilities	X
Claim on Bank 2	*+a2* *-a3*	Equity	X
Securities with Bank 2	X -a2		

securities settlement is simultaneous across all layers implies that the crediting of Investor 2's account with Bank 2 can only take place afterwards **(a3)** (Table 8.3).

The positions relating to the temporary extension of balance sheets caused by the disjunct settlement of the payment and security legs are shown in italics. These temporary IOUs create credit risk exposures despite settlement taking place in central bank money. **It could therefore be considered preferable to execute the securities transaction via DvP in commercial bank money** on the proviso that the CSD Bank attains a high credit rating.

8.5 Cross-Border Securities Custody: Example of Sanctions Against Russia

As explained in Sect. 8.3, a large share of securities settlement is cross-border, in the sense that end-investors and the issuer CSD are located in different parts of the world and currency areas. Indeed, portfolio diversification allows investors to improve the risk return characteristics of their portfolios, and as long as foreign investments are not considered to be subject to particular legal or expropriation risks, optimal securities portfolios will be globally diversified. For example, Euroclear (2021, 19) (the largest ICSD) explains:

> The Euroclear network comprises 2,000 financial institutions which use its platform to access 50 different markets and settle transactions in 50 currencies. On their behalf, the group holds €37.6 trillion of assets under custody, and enables over 276 million transactions per year, worth an equivalent of €1 quadrillion (1,000,000,000,000,000) or approximately 12.5 times world economic output.

International custodian banks like BNP Paribas, BNY Mellon, Citibank, Deutsche Bank etc. also provide international intermediation services to investors by providing access to a variety of CSDs, including via ICSDs. For example, BNP Paribas (2023) advertises its services in the international custody business as follows:

> Through our global clearing and settlement service we connect clients' trading activities to post-trade market infrastructures . . . Rarely considered an exciting part of our industry, trade settlement needs to work, efficiently and cost effectively. Whatever the size or the number of countries our clients operate in, we design solutions that meet their requirements . . . Our global custody offer covers over 90 markets working in perfect harmony with our proprietary local network and extended providers to give clients a seamless experience. Our augmented custody program leverages digital tools to bring greater efficiencies, such as a single way to provide SSI (standing settlement instructions) to our broker clients, better cut-offs for instructions and faster flow of information from local markets.

International securities holding chains can be very long and encompass several custodian banks This was reinforced by the difficulties in tracking some Russian foreign securities in order to freeze them as a G7 reaction to the Russian attack on Ukraine in February 2022. Russia's attack on Ukraine launched on 24 February 2022 was condemned as a brutal war of aggression by Western countries. For example, the European Council declared on 9 February 2023 that "Russia must stop this atrocious war immediately. The European Union will stand by Ukraine with its steadfast support as long as it takes". Western countries enacted sanctions and froze the financial assets of sanctioned Russian state entities and individuals, including the Central Bank of Russia. The central bank's foreign reserves were frozen by the sanctioning countries as of 28 February 2022. However, only 45 countries participated (including the USA, Canada, Australia, New Zealand, Japan, South Korea, Taiwan, Singapore, EU 27, UK, Switzerland, Norway, Island, North-Macedonia, Montenegro). Large economies with developed financial systems, such as Brazil, India, China, South Africa, Turkey, Mexico or Indonesia, did not participate.

According to the Belgian Government, Western sanctions have frozen €196.6bn in Russian assets at the ICSD Euroclear Bank, of which €180bn are Russian central bank assets (FT, Laura Dubois in Brussels May 24, 2023). This was despite the fact that Russia had since 2014 (i.e. following the invasion of the Crimea) already to some extent restructured their foreign assets in view of a deterioration of relations with the West. Michael Sandbu discussed in the Financial Times (9 March 2023, "Chasing Russia's shadow reserves—If you were Putin, where would you put your hard currency energy revenues?" Opinion/Free Lunch) Russia's problem to protect its remaining visible foreign reserves and those still generated via gas exports from additional sanctions:

> We can be sure that Moscow is thinking about how to put its unsanctioned cash pile, however big it is, beyond the reach of western jurisdiction. The Putin regime's operators understand that once Europe fully sheds its dependence on Russian energy, an important reason to limit sanctions will have gone. How to secure itself as far as possible against possible future sanctions would be the logical extension of Russia's work to reduce its vulnerabilities to western measures since its first invasion of Ukraine in 2014 . . . How might Moscow have gone about protecting its shadow reserves?.

In the fictitious financial accounts below, we start by assuming how the Central Bank of Russia (CBR) held its foreign reserves initially. **What global financial operations would CBR likely undertake to protect the reserves from potential Western sanctions?** Assume that initially the reserves are held in a G7 country, but Russia believes that this country will sanction these foreign currency claims (once it attacks a neighbouring country). Further, we include two third-countries for which Russia is confident that they will not participate in Western sanctions (i.e. a "non-sanctioning country"—NSC). We proceed on the following assumptions:

- Exchange rates between Russia, the two NSC countries and the G7 country are 1: 1:1:1 (hence, it is not necessary for exchange rate factors to be included).
- The settlement of G7 securities transactions take place at a CSD with a banking licence which settles in commercial bank money. However, we presume that deposits are uploaded to the CSD only for settlement and are transferred back by the recipient of the funds (the seller of the security) afterwards to the relevant bank. We do not show this transfer in- and out- of deposits to the CSD.
- Two correspondent banks are involved in the G7 country.
- CBR uses in total two NSCs as this allows the authorities to better blur any trace.
- CBR has foreign reserves of **A + B + C**, which it initially holds as follows: **"A"** in G7 securities, **"B"** as deposits in a nostro account with the G7 Bank 1, and **"C"** as deposits with the G7 central bank.

The CBR may apply the following sequence of financial transactions and payments to hide its foreign currency claims:

1. CBR sells its G7 securities held in the G7 country CSD to G7 Bank 1 and gets its nostro account with G7 Bank 1 credited **(a)**.

2. CBR instructs G7 Bank 1 to transfer the funds held on its nostro account (**which is now equal to "B + a"**) to NSC 1 Bank's nostro account with G7 Bank 2 **(a + b), with b = B.**
3. CBR instructs the G7 central bank to transfer its funds held with it to NSC 1 Bank's nostro account with G7 Bank 2 **(c).** CBR now holds all its foreign reserves as deposits on its nostro account with NSC 1 Bank. Of course, CBR could also have decided a different asset allocation (below we will indeed assume that the CBR diversifies again these assets).

In the example, it seems so far obvious where the money went, as the transfers still took place in Western systems, particularly if one can observe the related SWIFT messages. CBR could therefore, after this first round of transactions, continue to blur the traces of its reserves by initiating further transfers and securities transactions with other NSC banks/countries. Since the latter are no longer visible to any Western entity, this allows to make unknown to the Western parties where the funds of the CBR ended.

Assume that indeed the CBR:

4. Instructs NSC 1 Bank to transfer its entire correspondent bank account position **(d = a + b + c)** to NSC 2 Bank in NSC 2, with a correspondent transfer between the correspondent bank accounts at the G7 correspondent bank (we assume that the two NSC banks involved use the same G7 correspondent bank—i.e. G7 Bank 2).

In reality, the CBR will likely split amounts and distribute them over several banks, for the sake of being even less transparent and managing its credit risk exposure. The CBR can therefore reduce its credit risk exposure to NSC 2 Bank by diversifying its position into securities holdings, using the NSC 2 Bank as a custodian. To this end:

5. CBR instructs NSC 2 Bank to buy securities in the amount of "**e**" from G7 Bank 1 **(where e < d)** at the G7 CSD. NSC 2 Bank instructs its correspondent bank in the G7 country, G7 Bank 2 to pay the money from its correspondent account (by transferring it to the RTGS account of the CSD, for the benefit of G7 Bank 1).

In the accounts below, we show the balance sheet positions that are affected (in the interests of simplicity). The accounts also illustrate that the net cross-border financial positions of the different countries do not change because of these transactions, even if the visible gross bilateral positions change. For example, from the perspective of the G7 country, it can be observed that the gross cross-border claims of NSC 2 towards the G7 country have ultimately increased, while the NSC 1 position initially increased, and then declined. The difference of NSC 2's financial position towards the G7 country before and after the re-investment into G7 securities is not visible from the perspective of the G7 country as the custody chain is unknown to it. Still, strictly speaking the securities custody chain is only a custody chain, and the CBR has in principle no credit risk towards the custodian (only custody and legal

Table 8.4 Example of foreign reserve protection amid the application of sanctions

Russia			
Central Bank of Russia			
Deposits at G7 CB	C -c	Liabilities	X
Nostro at G7 Bank 1	B +a -a -b		
Securities at G7 CSD	A -a		
Deposits at G7 CSD			
Nostro at NSC 1 Bank	+a +b +c -d		
Nostro at NSC 2 Bank	+d -e		
Securities at NSC 2 Bank	+e		
G7 country			
G7 Bank 1			
Deposits at central bank	X -a -b	Vostro CBR	B +a -a -b
Deposits at CSD	X +e		
Securities account CSD	X +a -e		
G7 Bank 2			
Deposits at central bank	X +a +b +c -e	Vostro NSC 1 Bank	X +a +b +c -d
		Vostro NSC 2 Bank	X +d -e
G7 Central Bank			
Other assets	X	Deposits CBR	C -c
		Deposits G7 Bank 1	X -a -b +e
		Deposits G7 Bank 2	X +a +b +c -e
G7 CSD Bank			
Deposits at central bank	X	Sec. account CBR	A -a
Securities issued CSD	X	Sec. account G7 Bank 1	X +a -e
		Sec. account NSC 2 Bank	X +e
NSC 1			
NSC 1 Bank			
Nostro G7 Bank 2	X +a +b +c -d	Vostro CBR	+a +b +c -d
Securities at G7 CSD	X		
NSC 2			
NSC 2 Bank			
Nostro G7 Bank 2	X +d -e	Vostro CBR	+d -e
Sec. account G7 CSD	X +e	Securities account CBR	+e

risk) but is the owner of the G7 securities. This is different for deposit chains, which are actually no chains at all: the CBR has a claim against the NSC correspondent bank it uses, and what this bank does on its asset side to match that liability is only the business of this bank (Table 8.4).

As a variant to the last step, the re-investment could also be done in a way to lengthen the custody chain by a further step, by CBR not having the securities directly at NCS 2 Bank but asking NCS 2 Bank to hold the securities with NCS 1 Bank as a second custodian bank in the custody chain, with NCS 1 Bank then holding the securities with the G7 CSD. In this case, the second half of the above financial accounts would take the following form (Table 8.5):

8.6 TARGET2 Securities

An approach which enables securities settlement on a DvP basis in central bank money is through the euro area **T2S system**. In the strictest sense, T2S is not a SSS. Rather, it is a scheme where participating CSDs outsource their securities settlement

Table 8.5 Further lengthening of custody chains amid the application of sanctions

G7 CSD Bank			
Deposits at central bank	X	Sec. account CBR	A -a
Securities issued CSD	X	Sec. account G7 Bank 1	X +a -e
		Sec. account NSC 1 Bank	X +e
NSC 1			
NSC 1 Bank			
Nostro G7 Bank 2	X +a +b +c -d	Vostro CBR	+a +b +c -d
Securities at G7 CSD	X +e	Sec account NSC 2 Bank	+e
NSC 2			
NSC 2 Bank			
Nostro G7 Bank 2	X +d -e	Vostro CBR	+d -e
Sec. account NSC 1 Bank	+e	Securities account CBR	+e

operations to the T2S platform. T2S operates as an **integrated model**, but somewhat differs to the case considered above. That is to say, instead of central banks outsourcing the securities leg to CSDs, under **T2S CSDs outsource the delivery of securities to T2S**. Moreover, in contrast to CSDs controlling dedicated cash accounts for securities settlement on behalf of the central bank, **under T2S the settlement of any cash leg is completed through dedicated cash accounts maintained by T2S** (i.e. the central bank). T2S also employs an algorithm which enables cash settlement to be completed on a multilateral net basis (i.e. DvP model 3), as the T2S system is able to calculate the net cash positions of participants which allows a purchase of securities to occur using the liquidity gained from the sale of other securities. However, T2S also allows features an intraday-credit scheme which is carried out on an auto-collateralised basis (see e.g. ECB, 2022c).

Aside from the above features, one of the major innovations of T2S is that cross-border securities settlement becomes analogous to domestic settlement for members of the Eurosystem. Prior to T2S, participants were required to employ various CSDs or custodians to access different markets. Such hurdles have now been circumvented through the introduction of T2S, as now CSDs are "linked" via the T2S platform.

T2S is a technical service that does not have any assets or liabilities, nor does it maintain securities accounts (i.e. it is not a legal entity). The financial accounts representation below takes this into account, in which Investor 1 purchases some securities from Investor 2 in the amount of "a". The "area of control" of T2S is the one shown in grey. The T2S dedicated cash accounts (DCA) are central bank liabilities, while the securities accounts of banks belong to the CSD, but are outsourced and controlled by the central bank ensure DvP settlement. We assume that the banks have already sufficient liquidity in their T2S dedicated DCA for the settlement of the assumed securities transaction. Indeed, as of the changes implemented in March 2023, banks can permanently hold a liquidity pool in their T2S DCA—see below for a precise representation of the account structure of banks after the March 2023 changes. We also assume below that banks are comfortable with their position in their T2S DCA after the securities operation. In other words,

Table 8.6 DvP settlement with T2S (T2S control area is shaded in grey)

Investor 1			
Deposits at Bank 1	X -a	Other liabilities	X
Securities with Bank 1	X +a	Equity	X
Bank 1			
RTGS account with CB	X	Other liabilities	X
T2S DCA	X -a	Deposits Investor 1	X -a
Securities in CSD	X +a	Sec. account Investor 1	X +a
Other assets	X	Equity	X
Bank 2			
RTGS account with CB	X	Other liabilities	X
T2S DCA	X +a	Deposits Investor 2	X +a
Securities in CSD	X -a	Sec. account Investor 2	X -a
Other assets	X	Equity	X
Investor 2			
Deposits at Bank 2	X +a	Other liabilities	X
Securities with Bank 2	X -a	Equity	X
Eurosystem			
Other assets	X	Other liabilities	X
		Bank 1 RTGS account	X
		Bank 2 RTGS account	X
		T2S DCA Bank 1	X -a
		T2S DCA Bank 2	X +a
CSD			
Securities	X	Securities account Bank 1	X +a
Other assets	X	Securities account Bank 2	X -a
		Other Liabilities	X
		Equity	X

we do not cover below any funding operations or defunding operations in and out of DCA. We also assume that all bookings are done simultaneously across the client, bank, central bank and CSD layer (which is a simplification for the client layer) (Table 8.6).

In the accounts above, we assumed that the T2S DCA had already been pre-funded, such that no transfer was needed from the RTGS account to the T2S DCA for the bank (i.e. Bank 1) that needed to provide the payment leg in T2S. For the sake of completeness, it should be mentioned that as of March 2023, banks in T2 manage their liquidity from one central liquidity account, called a Main Cash Account (MCA) from which they fund and defund three DCAs, namely for RTGS, T2S and TIPS. The deposit facility offered in the context of the monetary policy operations framework can also be funded and defunded from the MCA. Therefore, strictly speaking the account structure of Bank 1 within the Eurosystem is as shown in the following accounts below, where we depict a funding operation in which Bank 1 first transfers "b" from its MCA to the T2S DCA, and following securities settlement—in which the T2S DCA of Bank 1 would be debited in the amount of "a" as shown above—a defunding operation transpires in which Bank 1 transfers "c" from its T2S DCA to its MCA (where b > a > c). Direct transfers between DCAs are prohibited (Table 8.7).

Table 8.7 Funding and defunding of Bank 1

Eurosystem			
Other assets	X	Other liabilities	X
		Bank 1 MCA	X -b +c
		Bank 1 RTGS DCA	X
		Bank 1 T2S DCA	X +b -c
		Bank 1 TIPS DCA	X
		Bank 1 deposit facility	X

T2S has been a success story: while participation of CSDs is voluntary, all major CSDs of the euro area have joined or are in the process of joining, driven by the desire of their clients to settle securities DvP in central bank money and using a single pool of liquidity (central bank money) instead of having segregated pools of commercial bank money with each CSD.

References

BdF. (2018). *Payments and market infrastructure in the digital age*. BdF Publication.

Bech, M. L., Hancock, J., & Wadsworth, A. (2020b). Central securities depositories and securities settlement systems. *BIS Quarterly Review*, March 2020.

Bech, M. L., Hancock, J., & Zhang, W. (2020c). Fast retail payment systems. *BIS Quarterly Review*, March.

Bech, M. L., Hancock, J., Rice, T., & Wadsworth, A. (2020d). On the future of securities settlement. *BIS Quarterly Review*, March.

BNP Paribas. (2023). *Clearing, settlement and custody*. Available at: https://securities.cib.bnpparibas/all-our-solutions/custody-clearing-cash/clearing-settlement-custody/

Chan, D., Fontan, F., Rosati, S., & Russo, D. (2007). *The securities custody industry*. ECB Occasional Paper No. 68.

Comotto, R. (2011). *The interconnectivity of central bank and commercial bank money in the clearing and settlement of the European repo market*. Compiled for the European Repo Council.

CPSS. (1992). *Delivery versus payment in securities settlement systems*. Bank of International Settlements, Basle.

CPSS. (1995). Cross-border securities settlement. Report prepared by the *Committee on Payment and Settlement Systems of the Central Banks of the Group of Ten Countries*, Bank of International Settlements, .

CPSS-IOSCO. (2012). *Principles for financial market infrastructures*. Bank of International Settlements.

Dickinson, K. (2015). *Financial markets operations management*. Wiley.

ECB. (2004). *The use of central bank money for settling securities transactions*. Frankfurt am Main, May 2004.

ECB. (2014). *Improvements to commercial bank money (COBM) settlement arrangements for collateral operations*. Frankfurt am Main, July 2014.

ECB. (2022c). *TARGET2-securities annual report 2021*. Frankfurt am Main, May 2022.

Emanuel, C. J. (1976). The expanding Eurobond market. *Finance and Development, 13*(3), 33.

Euroclear. (2021). *Annual report – Euroclear annual review 2021*. Available at: https://www.euroclear.com/investorrelations/en/annual-reports.html

Moles, P., & Terry, N. (1997). *The handbook of international financial terms*. Oxford University Press.

Mueller, W., M. (1910). The organization of credit and banking in arrangements in Germany (pp. 117–169). In *National Monetary Commission, Miscellaneous Articles on German Banking, 61st Congress, 2nd Session*. Government Printing Office, .
O'Malley, C. (2015). *Bonds without borders: A history of the Eurobond market*. Wiley.
Thomadakis, A. (2022). *Shortening the settlement cycle: Why Europe should not wait too long to introduce T + 1*. European Capital Markets Institute Commentary no 77.
Triffin, R. (1960). *Gold and the dollar crisis: The future of convertibility*. Yale University Press.
Van Cayseele, P., & Wuyts, C. (2007). Cost efficiency in the European securities settlement and depository industry. *Journal of Banking and Finance, 31*(10), 3058–3079.

Unbacked Crypto-Assets, Stablecoins and CBDC

9

9.1 Introduction

This chapter reviews three innovations in payments: **(1) unbacked crypto-assets; (2) stablecoins; and (3) CBDC**. Although of very different nature, they are often discussed together, which we will try to explain below after defining the key terms. The BIS (2022, Chap. 3) provides the following widely used definitions of key crypto concepts:

- **Cryptocurrency (also crypto-asset or crypto):** a type of private sector digital asset that depends primarily on cryptography and distributed ledger (or similar) technologies.
- **Distributed ledger technology (DLT):** a means of saving information through a distributed ledger, i.e. a repeated digital copy of data available at multiple locations.
- **Permissioned DLT:** a form of DLT whereby only a pre-defined group of trusted institutions can act as a validating node.
- **Permissionless DLT:** a form of DLT where any participant can act as a validating node, for instance with (permissionless) blockchains.
- **Stablecoin:** a cryptocurrency that aims to maintain a stable value relative to a specified asset (e.g. the USD), or a pool or basket of assets (e.g. special drawing rights).

Turning to the definition of CBDC, the ECB for example distinguishes in its digital euro glossary:

- **CBDC:** an electronically recorded monetary liability of the central bank.
- **retail CBDC:** a CBDC accessible to everyone, i.e. also to all parties outside the banking system such as citizens, businesses and government entities.

U. Bindseil, G. Pantelopoulos, *Introduction to Payments and Financial Market Infrastructures*, Springer Texts in Business and Economics,
https://doi.org/10.1007/978-3-031-39520-8_9

- **wholesale CBDC:** a CBDC accessible only to a narrow set of financial institutions and few other parties (governments, financial market infrastructures). Wholesale CBDC already exists in the form of RTGS (real time gross settlement) balances with central banks.

There are unfortunately several issues of ambiguity in the terminology First, diverging from the ECB definition above, many other central banks and the BIS have used the term "wholesale CBDC" for "wholesale CBDC based on DLT". This is confusing because the term "retail CBDC" is not meant to be linked to a certain technology—it is about granting any form of access to digital central bank monetary liabilities to the broader public. Second, many seem to use the term "digitalisation of money" when actually they mean "moving towards a DLT based system of recording a transfer of funds". Needless to say, central ledgers are today equally "digital", and a different approach to database architecture and consensus mechanisms is not making anything more "digital". Third, while stablecoins and unbacked crypto-assets share (according to the BIS definition) the technological feature of being based on DLT, they are functionally very different, and it is not clear why database architecture and consensus mechanism per se should matter so much if public policy issues around these very different constructs are being discussed (e.g. by public sector regulators, from a financial stability perspective). For instance, all the concerns that were raised by the public sector regarding Facebook's global stablecoin project "Libra" (later renamed "Diem") had nothing to do with its planned underlying DLT technology. It would also have prevailed if Libra would have not referred to technology at all in its announcements, but only to its functional ambitions, or if it would have envisaged to implement it without DLT, but on the basis of standard central ledger based technology (like other global retail payment endeavours, such as PayPal). Eventually, stablecoins denominated in currency units, issued by an issuer and backed with assets, are functionally close to e-money constructs (which are required to be convertible and to be fully backed by highly liquid assets, typically deposits with a bank). According to Article 2(2) of the EU e-money Directive (2009/110/EC), "electronic money" means "electronically, including magnetically, stored monetary value as represented by a claim on the issuer which is issued on receipt of funds for the purpose of making payment transactions...and which is accepted by a natural or legal person other than the electronic money issuer".

In contrast, unbacked crypto-assets like Bitcoin or Ethereum that operate via a permissionless blockchain are truly innovative, not only from the perspective of technology, but also with regards to the financial object they create. The original nature of these financial objects has to be acknowledged, even if one would come to the conclusion that these are neither suitable as store of value (as their value is highly unstable), nor as means of payment and settlement.

What unbacked crypto-assets and stablecoins share *so far* is that they are today both predominantly used in the same universe—the crypto investment universe—whereby stablecoins provide a bridge between the unbacked crypto-asset world and the central bank and commercial bank money world. Stablecoins are the means of payment integrated into crypto trading platforms. Stablecoin projects such as Libra/ Diem had much larger ambitions, namely to serve both as retail means of payment and store of value for anyone (without any necessary involvement in crypto-asset investment).

9.2 Unbacked Crypto-Assets

9.2.1 Bitcoin

In 2007 a group of software developers introduced a completely decentralised booking concept (Schar & Berentsen, 2020; Bindseil et al., 2022). Operating under the pseudonym Satoshi Nakamoto, a white paper and source code for "digital cash" were published (Nakamoto, 2008). In January 2008, the first fifty Bitcoins were generated. The Bitcoin system permits holders of Bitcoin to remain anonymous via encryption. At the same time, the Bitcoin blockchain is transparent in the sense that it is public knowledge what addresses hold which amounts of Bitcoin. Participants can also observe the related transaction flows etc. Transfers are conceived as irreversible, irrespective of the reason (which however does not preclude that on the basis of civil law, someone could claim back crypto assets and try to enforce a transfer back, effectively reversing a transfer).

Further remarkable functional and organisational features of Bitcoin are:

- As opposed to some form of central counterparty or issuer, no central authority keeps the system stable. Rather, a global network of computers control, monitor and store information—being all automatic incentives to support the stability of the system.
- New Bitcoins are coined by users acting as "miners", and new data packets—or "blocks"—are added to the blockchain every few minutes.
- The maximum number of Bitcoins is limited to approximately 21 million, whereby around 19 million are already in circulation as of 2022.
- To prove the validity of the entire blockchain and its extensions, computers solve a mathematical puzzle for each block—the "proof-of-work" mechanism. The so-called miners validate the transactions by entering them into a public ledger. Currently rewards include transaction fees as well as seignorage from newly created Bitcoins, i.e. the market value of a Bitcoin minus the mining costs.

The updated blockchain is shared amongst all participants in the public ledger. The accounts below illustrate the transaction between two persons in exchange for real goods (be it a Pizza at a restaurant that would accept Bitcoin, or an illegal weapon bought on the dark web). We include the factor "α" which is the inverse of the price of a Bitcoin relative to currency A at the moment of the transaction which is equal to the value of "a". Since settlement of the transaction is not DvP, the transaction is subject to temporary IOUs and settlement risk, which are however

Table 9.1 Payment in bitcoin: no service providers

Eurosystem			
Other assets	X	Other liabilities	X
		Bank 1 MCA	X -b +c
		Bank 1 RTGS DCA	X
		Bank 1 T2S DCA	X +b -c
		Bank 1 TIPS DCA	X
		Bank 1 deposit facility	X

not shown in the accounts below for the sake of simplicity. Moreover, the accounts do not show the minting of new Bitcoins in the context of the validation of the block in which the transfer is included. Also, one could argue that the Bitcoin network actually has no true balance sheet as Bitcoins are not a liability of any counterparty (Table 9.1).

The striking feature of payments in Bitcoin is that, as pledged by Nakamoto (2008), no financial intermediaries need to provide their balance sheet for Bitcoin transactions to happen, nor are any traditional infrastructures, intermediaries, or payment systems required. The payment occurs directly in a commodity-like asset and can be completed in accordance with the frequency of its settlement cycles. **A major drawback of the use of Bitcoin as means of payment is in any case its price instability.**

The proof-of-work method to validate new blocks of the blockchain has a scalable difficulty level and aims to keep the incentive for miners to keep running the system sufficiently high. Since Bitcoin prices directly affects the value of the mined coins, the amount of resources miners have to spend on mining is scaled through adjusting the complexity of the encryption puzzle that needs to be solved by miners (see e.g. the simple model of de Vries, 2021). As a consequence, increasing bitcoin prices imply that miners require more electricity to solve the puzzle and consume more electricity and increase carbon emissions. Therefore, the environmental cost of Bitcoin is proportional to its price, which illustrates Bitcoin's unfortunate inherent inefficiency.

Beyond energy consumption, **several authors have raised concerns on Bitcoin's underlying technology and concept** (see e.g. Taleb, 2021; Avoca, 2021; Acemoglu, 2021; Kolbert, 2021). First, the proof-of-work concept, which is a constituting feature of the Bitcoin system, is generally recognised as cumbersome and slow. Second, slow and opaque pricing networks have traditionally attracted predatory high-frequency algorithm traders and are vulnerable to related market stress. Third, for example Avoca (2021) argues that the Bitcoin network is also vulnerable because of its reliance on a single security technology that experts consider to be outdated by advances in computing (e.g. Bitcoin uses the secure hash algorithm (SHA) which is more than 20 years old).

For all its shortcomings, advocates of Bitcoin suggest that it restores freedom from government control and from centralized entities that abuse their power and would enable "decentralized finance" (DeFi). DeFi would bring the financial emancipation of the individual and the ultimate democratization of the monetary system (see also the following section). Yet it can be disputed that handing over power to computers can be considered to be democratisation or liberation. It would seem more democratic to run market infrastructure through mutualist governance, or under the control of democratically elected governments. The observed governance, operational and organisational structure of payment and FMIs, including the layering, distributed nodes and central institutions (which themselves can be state owned, mutual firms, or capitalist firms) is likely to be an outcome of the search for economic efficiency and stability. It seems counterintuitive that uncontrolled, autonomous, computer-governed payment systems are preferable from any perspective, including the one of democracy and liberty.

Moderate advocates of Bitcoin (e.g. Malekan, 2022) have noted that at least in countries subject to dictatorship and repression, Bitcoin provides a means of payment and store of value outside the control of the government. For example, the opposition and citizens of Iran, Afghanistan, Russia or Venezuela could regain some liberty and power thanks to Bitcoin. However, this argument can be reversed: the freedom of women in Iran gained by Bitcoin is mirrored by the one gained by drug dealers and cyber criminals in democratic open societies. The argument would therefore require that the use of Bitcoin could be limited to non-democratic countries.

Furthermore, although in its original guise Bitcoin was envisaged as a decentralised means of payment and settlement, **the actual mechanics of payment and settlement in Bitcoin normally rely on centralised profit-oriented companies.** As Poon and Dryja (2016) note (amongst others), the inefficiency of settling small payments on the Bitcoin blockchain is often addressed by offloading transactions to a large custodian, which settles the payments between clients in its own books (e.g. like in El Salvador within the Chivo Wallet). But this requires trusting the custodian, accepting related risks and possibly to pay the custodian a fee. It also betrays the ideology behind decentralized finance and Bitcoin.

This mixed approach often encountered in reality is exhibited below in Table 9.2. In this example, each trader relies on a separate crypto-asset service provider (CASP). Settlement is now followed by Person 2 accruing a claim on a counterparty, the Bitcoin CASP. In this way, the more recent ambitious attempts to make Bitcoin a means of payment (e.g. in El Salvador) goes against its foundational principles, including the core idea of Nakamoto (2008) to overcome the role of central intermediaries.

Unbacked crypto assets also offer a vision of a global means of payment without national jurisdictions to overcome borders (in contrast with conventional cross-border payments). While indeed a network like Bitcoin can be used equivalently for global payments, it needs also to be taken into account that the high cost of conventional cross-border payments is not due to the supposed inefficiency of central ledger-based payment instruments per se, but is attributable (to a large extent) to the costs of regulatory requirements (e.g. KYC, AML/CFT etc.). Regulators should impose the same level of scrutiny on international Bitcoin transfers from

Table 9.2 One CASP issuing bitcoin deposits

Country A (in A currency)			
Person 1			
Real goods	X +a	Equity	X
Bitcoin deposits	X -a		
Bank deposits	X		
Bitcoin CASP			
Bitcoin	X	Person 1	X -a
Other assets	X	Person 2	X +a
Bank deposits	X	Equity	X
Bitcoin network (in Bitcoin)			
Total minted bitcoins	X	Bitcoin of CASP	X
		Other bitcoin	X
Person 2			
Real goods	X -a	Equity	X
Bitcoin deposits	X +a		
Bank deposits	X		

the AML/CFT perspective as otherwise the effectiveness of AML/CFT regulation would be undermined (as illegal transactions migrate to the Bitcoin network, as currently tends to be the case). Therefore, this supposed comparative advantage of Bitcoin would tend to disappear.

Overall, it is difficult to avoid the conclusion that despite the idealistic vision behind Bitcoin, and the impressiveness of its technology achievement, the true reason for the ongoing hype around Bitcoin is the dream of Bitcoin speculators to get rich by holding Bitcoin and benefitting from significant price increases, such as those culminating in the 2021 price peak. The popular phrase that Bitcoiners use towards sceptics of "have fun staying poor" may unfortunately summarise the spirit of today's Bitcoin community. The other narratives justifying Bitcoin may have been meant seriously at first, but appear today more and more as distractions and pretention.

9.2.2 Decentralised Finance, Ethereum and Business Applications of Blockchain and DLT

Coinbase enthusiastically defines decentralised finance as follows (Coinbase website, 2 January 2023):

> DeFi (or "decentralized finance") is an umbrella term for financial services on public blockchains, primarily Ethereum. With DeFi, you can do most of the things that banks support — earn interest, borrow, lend, buy insurance, trade derivatives, trade assets, and more — but it's faster and doesn't require paperwork or a third party. As with crypto generally, DeFi is global, peer-to-peer (meaning directly between two people, not routed through a centralized system), pseudonymous, and open to all. ... DeFi takes the basic

> premise of Bitcoin — digital money — and expands on it, creating an entire digital alternative to Wall Street, but without all the associated costs (think office towers, trading floors, banker salaries). This has the potential to create more open, free, and fair financial markets that are accessible to anyone with an internet connection.

This vision could appear as an over-promise across many dimensions, and nothing of it has really turned close to reality so far (or has a reasonable probability of doing so). It also seems contradictory that this eulogy of DeFi is provided by a conventional, centralised, capitalist firm, Coinbase, which wants to provide intermediation services between human reality and the outlined DeFi vision. IOSCO (2022, 1) more neutrally defines that "DeFi commonly refers to the provision of financial products, services, arrangements and activities that use distributed ledger technology ("DLT") in an effort to disintermediate and decentralize legacy ecosystems by eliminating the need for some traditional financial intermediaries and centralized institutions." DeFi use cases include for example crypto-asset exchange, lending and borrowing, derivatives, crowd funding, and payments.

DeFi activities normally rely on systems built on public permissionless smart contract platforms, with the Ethereum blockchain being most common. The underlying blockchain provides the settlement layer. Smart contracts and auxiliary software create financial products and services (protocols) relying on this settlement layer. The Ethereum blockchain is permissionless like the Bitcoin one, but in addition allows the integration of smart contracts. Ethereum moved in 2022 from the highly inefficient proof-of-work mechanism to "proof-of-stake". De Vries (2021) estimates that the switch of mechanism allowed a reduction in energy consumption by at least 99.84%, illustrating how bad the efficiency of proof-of-work is. In principle, Ethereum could also be used as means of payment, but again like Bitcoin it suffers from a high price volatility (e.g. as witnessed in early 2022).

Smart contracts are code deployed to and executed on a blockchain, and provide the DeFi functionality (e.g. IOSCO, 2022, 6). Every DeFi solution relies on multiple smart contracts to form a specific protocol. On Ethereum, the software code that defines the smart contract is stored and executed on the blockchain. Ethereum miners charge a fee (in ETH) for every transaction, including transactions that trigger smart contracts. This fee also provides incentives against abuse consumption of network resources.

There have also been notable other innovations in the blockchain-sphere. Moving away from the vision of public and permissionless blockchains, there are now a number of "permissioned" (or "private") blockchain related projects like Hyperledger Fabric and R3 Corda. Hyperledger Fabric is governed by the Linux foundation and Corda by a company, R3. Both are not unbacked crypto-assets but blockchains. For example, the **Corda blockchain** is an open-source platform that promises easy management of legal contracts and other shared data between mutually trusting organizations. The platform would make it possible for a diverse range of applications to interoperate on a single network. R3 launched Corda as a platform for enabling services in the financial sector (Brown, 2018). Corda would also allow high privacy and security standards. R3 also offers the usual support by a software vendor, such as a commercial distribution platform, 24/7 support, and predictable release schedules. Corda offers various solutions for payments and market infrastructure issues. For example, Corda would allow for the entire life cycle of digital securities to be managed on a permissioned shared ledger allowing digital assets to move freely between counterparties, while maintaining regulatory compliance and keeping counterparties synchronized with the evolution of the asset over time. Corda would also act as a trusted bridge between the established infrastructure and the new world of distributed finance. It would automate and streamline the reconciliation process because it would deliver an immutable "single source of truth" for multiple parties. Transactions could be cryptographically signed and stored only by relevant parties to prevent exposing sensitive data. There is a multitude of other companies and initiatives which promise to improve payments or market infrastructure through blockchain technology, such as e.g. Ripple, which promises that its particular blockchain technology reduces the costs of remittances etc. whilst still ensuring reliability (see also AMI-SeCo, 2021).

9.2.3 The Crypto Winter of 2022

The year 2022 saw a number of setbacks in the crypto (i.e. DLT/blockchain) technology in payments and finance, each of which was of a very different nature:

- **Libra/Diem project given up in January 2022:** as the most ambitious and prominent attempt to have DLT/blockchain technology revolutionise payments, Libra had been launched in 2019 by Facebook (see below the subsection on stablecoins) "motivated by the desire to deliver substantial benefits to consumers and businesses, along with a payments solution for those who are currently underserved or excluded altogether from the traditional financial system". Its closure was announced end January 2022, blaming mainly signals from US "federal regulators that the project could not move ahead" (Diem, 2022).
- **Decline in the price of Bitcoin and of other unbacked crypto-assets during 2022**: the value of Bitcoin peaked at USD 69,000 in November 2021, but fell to USD 17,000 by mid-June 2022 staying there for the rest of the year, implying that many who had bought Bitcoin with the aim to benefit from ever increasing prices ended with large losses. At the same time, those who had been buying Bitcoin earlier and had sold their holdings at peak levels in 2021 made a fortune. In the absence of any fair value of Bitcoin, one may argue that Bitcoin is not suitable as investment and that investments into it could better be classified as gambling and be regulated accordingly (Seeman, 2022).
- **Failure of algorithmic stablecoins like Terra USD in May 2022** (see e.g. DNB, 2022, Box 1): Algorithmic stablecoins are issued in a decentralised way similar to an unbacked crypto-asset. Terra USD was issued by exchanging it for an unbacked crypto-asset named Luna. The Luna Foundation Guard – a non-profit

entity which was allocated a large amount of LUNA – could indirectly steer the issuance and redemption of USTC by selling and buying LUNA, because 1 USD worth of LUNA could be exchanged for 1 USTC and vice versa. As demand for USTC rose, the LUNA Foundation sold LUNA and used the receipts to subsidise a crypto investment – a scheme effectively close to a Ponzi scheme. Early investors benefitted from late investors who lost almost all their money. At its peak on 5 April 2022, LUNA had a market cap of USD 41 billion, while outstanding USTC peaked at USD 18.7 billion. Following broader price decreases in the crypto market, widespread withdrawals of USTC deposits caused panic and USTC lost its peg to the dollar. LUNA and USTC lost more than 90% of their market caps.
- **Failure of major crypto exchange FTX:** FTX was a Bahama based crypto exchange which had more than one million clients and was the third largest in the world in terms of volume. It filed for bankruptcy after critical articles on its business model and Ponzi-scheme like practices were published and large customer withdrawals could no longer be met. On 11 November, FTX filed for bankruptcy, and Sam Bankman Fried stepped down as CEO. On 12 November, FTX announced that a hack had drained the firm of $659 m, which had caused them to halt withdrawals. Aside from the hack, FTX was said to be unable to account for $1b-$2b of client funds. Its balance sheet showed liabilities of around 9 bn USD against assets of less than 1 billion USD.
- **Collapse of NFT market:** a nonfungible token is supposed to confirm unique ownership of a digital asset, using DLT/blockchain technology. They have been used for instance for digital art and collectibles ("Bored Ape Yacht Club" and "CryptoPunks" being two once highly valued digital art series). In early 2022, NFT art collection achieved record valuations with an estimated market cap of 17 billion, losing however again 95% of that value by October 2022.
- **In November 2022 the Australian Stock Exchange ASX gave up its project to migrate its settlement infrastructure to blockchain technology, writing off more than USD 165 million of project costs:** the project had been launched in 2016 to renew the existing Clearing House Electronic Subregister System (CHESS). The renewal should have allowed, thanks to blockchain and DLT, an acceleration of settlement times and a reduction of costs, with a plan to go live in 2018. Instead, it was delayed several times and given up in 2022 after a negative independent review by the consultancy firm Accenture. As noted by del Castillo and Paz (2022): the "cancellation is the latest setback among global exchanges looking to leverage blockchain, and a number of other efforts to implement permissioned versions of the open technology popularized by bitcoin ... The cancellation is a long fall from the heady days of 2016, when ASX's project was heralded as the flagship of institutional adoption of blockchain, helping its technology partner, New York-based Digital Asset Holdings, raise $307 million from JPMorgan, Goldman Sachs, and International Business Machines."

The future will tell which elements of crypto-assets and decentralised finance will recover and eventually provide value for society.

9.3 Stablecoins

9.3.1 Some Stablecoin Initiatives

The term "stablecoin" was first used in the White Paper of the "Dai Stablecoin System" (MakerDAO, 2017), which outlined that:

> Popular digital assets such as Bitcoin (BTC) and Ether (ETH) are too volatile to be used as everyday currency. The value of a bitcoin often experiences large fluctuations, rising or falling by as much as 25% in a single day and occasionally rising over 300% in a month. The Dai Stablecoin is a collateral-backed cryptocurrency whose value is stable relative to the US Dollar. We believe that stable digital assets like Dai Stablecoin are essential to realizing the full potential of blockchain technology.

The next project using the term stablecoin was **Havven**, which was a so-called "algorithmic" coin project (Brooks et al., 2018). The vision of Havven was to make supply endogenous, so as to stabilize the purchasing power of money. Section 1.3 of its whitepaper explained that:

> Stablecoins are cryptocurrencies designed for price stability. They should ideally be as effective at making payments as fiat currencies like the US Dollar, while retaining their other desirable properties. A decentralised payment network built on a stablecoin would be able to capture all the benefits of a permissionless system, while also eliminating volatility. One approach to achieving price stability is to produce a token whose price targets the value of a fiat currency.

Today's biggest stablecoin in terms of market capitalisation is **Tether** which claims to provide "individuals and organizations with a robust and decentralized method of exchanging value while using a familiar accounting unit" (Tether, 2016). Tether has become a common means of putting funds into and out of crypto trading platforms. The Whitepaper of Tether of 2016 ("Tether: Fiat currencies on the Bitcoin blockchain") explains that:

> The innovation of blockchains is an auditable and cryptographically secured global ledger. Asset backed token issuers and other market participants can take advantage of blockchain technology, along with embedded consensus systems, to transact in familiar, less volatile currencies and assets. In order to maintain accountability and to ensure stability in exchange price, we propose a method to maintain a one-to-one reserve ratio between a cryptocurrency token, . . . and its associated real world asset, fiat currency.

In the meantime, the most ambitious global stablecoin project was **Libra, launched by Facebook** in 2019 through a white paper (Libra, 2019). The Libra Association's mission was "to enable a simple global payment system and financial infrastructure that empowers billions of people", i.e. making Libra a global retail payment instrument, going much beyond existing stablecoins which played a role only as a bridge to the crypto investment space. Libra was to be implemented via its own blockchain and was to be fully backed by a reserve of various assets (bank deposits and short-term government securities). Libra's governance mechanism was designed as a consortium (the "Libra Association") including big-name companies such as Mastercard, PayPal, Visa, Stripe, eBay, Coinbase, Uber and others. Facebook itself was "expected to maintain a leadership role." The social media giant also planned to maintain its influence by running a wallet, Calibra. While the first white paper put focus on a single global Libra coin being a weighted basked of major international currencies, the second white paper (Libra, 2020) put more emphasis on single-currency stablecoins in US dollars (USD), British pounds (GBP), euro (EUR) and Singapore dollars (SGD). In the Libra Reserve, custodian banks hold assets on behalf of the Libra Association backing the single-currency stablecoins. The asset backing would be composed as follows: over 80% were to be invested in short-term securities (up to 3 months remaining maturity) issued by liquid sovereigns with low credit risk (i.e. A+ rating from S&P and A1 from Moody's, or higher). The remainder was to be held in cash, with overnight transfers into money market funds. In the view of push-back by regulators, the Libra (Diem) project was closed in January 2022.

While Libra (Diem) was the most ambitious stablecoin initiative so far in the area of *retail* payments (notably for P2P and e-commerce), an ambitious *wholesale* stablecoin is **Fnality**. Founded in 2019, Fnality aims at using stablecoins backed by central bank money to settle payments, DvP and PvP transactions on a permissioned blockchain. Fnality was set up by a consortium of global financial institutions who initially wished to explore how blockchain and DLT could use tokenised cash assets to settle securities trades such as to alleviate the challenges posed by conventional FMIs. Initially under the name Utility Settlement Coin (USC) Project, it pursued the objective of the creation of a peer-to-peer digital cash asset to settle tokenised transactions with finality. The payment solution was meant to be available in multiple currencies to allow members an integrated management of global liquidity. It also was designed to be capable of inter-operating across multiple business platforms, whether to support PvP or DvP settlement of financial transactions.

9.3.2 Policy Issues and Regulation of Stablecoins

From the moment when Facebook appeared with its Libra (later Diem) project, international standard setters and regulators have devoted a high degree of attention to stablecoins, starting with the report of the G7 working group on stablecoins (2019). In this report, the international regulatory community endorses that stablecoins are something very different and promising for improving payments, and in particular global payments (p. ii):

> Stablecoins have many of the features of cryptoassets but seek to stabilise the price of the "coin" by linking its value to that of a pool of assets. Therefore, stablecoins might be more capable of serving as a means of payment and store of value, and they could potentially contribute to the development of global payment arrangements that are faster, cheaper and more inclusive than present arrangements.

At least from today's perspective, **underlying technology (distributed ledger or similar) should not make such a difference per se from a regulatory perspective**. From any public policy perspective, be it payment system policies, monetary policy, financial stability, or consumer protection, the underlying IT technology for validating and recording transfers of funds should not matter per se—as long as it is effective and secure. From a functional perspective, a global payment instrument can be based either on DLT and blockchain or on central ledger technology (with many variants of storage and validation techniques), with each probably having their specific advantages in some circumstances, and not excluding that in the future, DLT technology may play a much bigger role than it does today.

If one could identify specific reasons why DLT and blockchain technology would per se matter from a micro or macro-prudential perspective, then certain elements of regulating the related payment instruments should focus on technology. However, despite all the work of regulators for the last 3 years to develop regulation for stablecoins, very little has been identified that really relates to technology. **Regulators and standard setters, despite having defined stablecoins as being based on cryptographic technology such as DLT, do not come back to technology when developing regulatory considerations**. At the international level, work on stablecoin regulation is taking place through the BIS, G20, G7, FSB, IOSCO, BCBS, FATF, CPMI and other groups. Publications through the G7 (2019) or CPMI-IOSCO (2021) do not explore links between the supposed definitory technology of stablecoins (cryptography and DLT or similar) and regulatory issues. Instead, all issues discussed would seem to be applicable to a central ledger-based "conventional" global payment institution. As Panetta (2020) notes "Just like any other payment system or scheme, if liquidity, settlement, operational and cyber risks are not properly managed, they may threaten the functioning of stablecoin arrangements and lead to systemic instability."

How can we explain the contradiction that on one side regulators devote enormous attention to a supposed new class of payment arrangements defined by technology, while then suggesting that technology would not matter for regulation? Why was the usual principle abandoned to address all similar payment endeavours, regardless of their underlying IT database and validation architecture, through one regulatory approach, leaving technology to the operational risk management where it will matter? Several explanations could be relevant:

- **Perception that DLT/blockchain would have huge potential as technology for payments**. Seeing the momentum in crypto-asset prices, and the enthusiasm around decentralised finance, authorities may have found the narratives of stablecoin issuers plausible in 2019 that their reliance on crypto-technology, DLT and blockchain would make a huge difference. Concretely, Libra/Diem seems to have been perceived as credible project to conquer global payments, undermine the role of central banks, the existing payment industry, and monetary sovereignty. Libra/Diem's narrative heavily relied on the superiority of blockchain technology and decentralisation for improving payments (the first

White Paper of Libra was indeed called "The Libra Blockchain" in 2019, referred to technology even in its title, and the name "Libra" promoted the false narrative of a "liberation" through decentralised finance). By believing that the technology underpinning stablecoins is highly credible (although with some risks), regulators may have believed that while functionally equivalent to existing non-DLT based payment instruments, they will take a fundamentally larger scale and thereby raise proportionally larger policy issues, creating an impetus for regulatory initiatives. Scared by the vision of an extremely successful Libra/Diem, worries of authorities around stablecoins also had a lot to do with risks of facilitating capital flows and undermining monetary sovereignty. Still today, effective stablecoin projects remain limited in terms of their success to serve as bridge between the world of speculation in unbacked crypto-assets and the normal payment and financial system, i.e. have not yet proven successful in domestic, let alone international payments. Regarding the latter, it needs to be reminded that the problems that cross-border payments face, such as high compliance costs and legal risks, will affect regulated stablecoins in the same way as they affect any other (equivalently regulated) payment instrument.

- **Initial impression that there could be stablecoins which would not be backed by assets**. So-called "algorithmic", i.e. unbacked stablecoins were initially considered to have sufficient plausibility to at least not be directly rejected as nonsense by authorities. If they would have been viable, such algorithmic stablecoins would indeed have been astonishing innovations and would have been quite different from existing payment instruments which rely on the idea of a 100% backing by liquid assets. In the meantime, algorithmic stablecoins are considered unviable (e.g. Panetta, 2022). After the fall of Terra/Luna in 2022, regulators have given up on including algorithmic stablecoins in what they consider viable and limit the emerging regulatory perimeter to fully backed and convertible stablecoins.
- **Initial impression that stablecoins would need no issuer.** Regulators may have thought that stablecoins could be organised as decentralised organisations on permissionless blockchains, such as Bitcoin, without any responsible issuer. Again, that would have made them highly innovative, and would have raised questions how to apply existing regulatory frameworks to them. However, the vision of a stablecoin without issuer seems remote.

None of these initial assumptions would merit today a singular approach to stablecoin regulation. Underlying IT technology does not seem to modify the nature, function or balance sheet logic of the payment instrument. Whether DLT and blockchain will be an absolute game changer for the potential success and scale of private issuers of global means of payment will be seen but does not change this conclusion. If a game changer, this only implies that effective regulation of global e-money payment institutions becomes even more important, regardless of what technology they are based on.

In sum, regulators could consider revisiting the approach to stablecoin regulation and instead of fragmenting regulation subsume the case of stablecoins under a functional regulation of payment institutions aiming at large scale and global reach. Only where technology would really be identified to make a difference from the public policy perspective should specific regulatory provision for technology be considered.

This conclusion neither questions the potential merits of blockchain and DLT to serve payments, nor that there is a risk that global payment giants could undermine financial stability, monetary sovereignty, or at least could abuse their market power at the detriment of citizens and firms. Regulation, supervision and oversight of payment institutions and instruments will remain highly relevant and significant efforts of public authorities are justified. Restructuring these efforts and avoiding fragmentation of regulation will benefit regulatory efficiency and consistency.

9.4 Central Bank Digital Currency

9.4.1 Introduction

The pros and cons of central bank digital currencies (CBDC) have been debated intensively since 2016 and now almost every central bank in the world seems on its way getting ready to one day issue CBDC. As mentioned at the beginning of the chapter, it has become common to distinguish between **"retail CBDC" and "wholesale CBDC"**, whereby the latter is used by many (including the BIS) in a somewhat confusing manner, for "wholesale CBDC involving new technologies such as DLT, blockchain and tokenisation". The questions that arise in the context of wholesale CBDC are the ones arising in the context of stablecoins in the sphere of private money: are these new underlying IT database and consensus/data validation mechanisms game changers that allow the efficiency of payments to be significantly improved, and even if they do so, is it a reason to assume that also functionally we are entering a new world with such technologies? Our tentative answer would be, also in the case of wholesale CBDC, that (i) so far it still has to be shown that such technology can per se lead to exceptional efficiency gains; (ii) even if it does, this would not per se change the logic of central bank money and its functional and monetary policy terms. Most of the time, it appears after some analysis that many properties that are typically assigned to DLT like 24/7 or "programmability" can also be achieved in centralised systems with a single ledger and non-decentralised consensus mechanism. Where permissionless blockchains and DLT seem to offer advantages is in terms of a decentralised ability to add code and functionality and to integrate easily DvP and PvP atomicity with various conditionalities for specific applications.

In the following, we therefore focus on **retail CBDC:** providing electronic central bank money to everyone and ending the current approach that only banks can access central bank money electronically, while all others need to be content with central bank money in paper format.

9.4.2 Reasons for Issuing Retail CBDC and Opposition

Central bankers have often motivated their work on CBDC mainly with the idea of preserving the advantages of central bank money in a digital age in which people may want to pay less and less with banknotes. Essentially, the availability and use of central bank money has served economies and societies well. Sticking exclusively with seventeenth century technology, paper notes, despite having also observed for decades now the replacement of all other paper forms of financial instruments (cheques, bills of exchange, paper promissory notes, paper form securities, etc), appears only at first conservative. Continuing to rely exclusively on paper money would actually be revolutionary, as it would imply to largely give up the well-tested two-layer monetary system based on a co-existence for everyone of central bank and commercial bank money. The advantages of preserving the universal access to central bank money also in a digital age include the following:

- The continued availability of an ultimate risk-free medium of settlement to novate all claims on parties of lesser credit quality and thereby preventing the build-up of complex IOU networks.
- Maintaining relevant the convertibility promise defining commercial bank money, which is essentially a promise to convert a claim at any time into central bank money.
- Have available for citizens a digital means of payment designed from a public preference perspective, and not only from a profit perspective. Money and payments are a function of universal importance for a society built on the division of labour. As argued by Simmel (1900), it is even at the very core of modern society.
- The availability and usability of central bank money adds to competition in an industry with network effects and thus typically a predominance of few players which will unavoidably try to abuse their market power.

Central bank money in the form of banknotes is sufficiently effective as long as banknotes are significantly used, such as to sustain the network effects underlying any successful means of payment. However, there is a trend towards less and less use of banknotes in retail payments and it seems easy to predict that in one or two decades, payments in banknotes will be unusual in most countries in the world. Progress on the side of mobile devices, electronic identity, biometrics and electronic payments will continue and tilt the balance of attractiveness further and further towards electronic payments. Not providing CBDC would then mean accepting to end the role of central bank money in retail payments because of not being ready in the twenty-first century to move away from seventeenth century technology. This does not imply that central banks should discontinue the issuance of banknotes, which retain for the foreseeable future some specific advantages in terms of inclusiveness, cyber resilience, and privacy, and accordingly central banks working on CBDC have stressed that they will not stop issuing banknotes.

Some have supported CBDC as it would allow to easily implement "sovereign money" In a sovereign money framework, banks would be crowded out in one way or the other from the issuing of means of payments. Banks would have to finance through longer term deposits and capital market instruments. Those advocating CBDC from this perspective perceive a number of advantages of sovereign money, such as (i) improved financial stability, (ii) preventing subsidising the banking system through bail outs with taxpayer money (through an implicit ex ante commitment not to do so); (iii) having citizens benefit from increased seignorage income resulting from an increased monetary base. One might also argue that a single layer monetary system is more efficient, and if it can be done from a technology perspective, it should in principle be preferable. Central banks have rejected these arguments as they continue to believe in a two-layer monetary system with an important role for commercial bank money and a relatively lean central bank balance sheet.

Opponents of CBDC still seem to regard paper banknotes as the universal and eternal form of central bank money accessible to all , and the idea to grant dematerialised access to central bank money to citizens as highly innovative and dangerous. However, history tells us the opposite: open access to central bank accounts is not new and preceded banknotes by two and a half centuries (from 1401 to 1661), and actually has been considered the *less* dangerous form of central bank money from the financial stability perspective for the subsequent three centuries (from 1664 to around 1950). As reviewed in Roberds and Velde (2014), Ugolini (2017), or Bindseil (2019), the first public banks issuing a means of payment—i.e. the earliest central banks—did so in the form of deposits, and not in the form of banknotes. Before the Stockholm Banco invented modern banknotes in 1661, there had been at least six major early public central banks that successfully issued giro deposits which were extensively used as means of payment. These public banks granted the possibility to open deposit accounts in principle to anyone, i.e. granted universal access to central bank liabilities (such as banknotes do, and such as CBDC would). However, in the absence of electronic remote access, reach was limited to those who could come to the bank to undertake their transactions physically.

Opponents of CBDC have voiced two types of concerns with regards to CBDC, namely of a "fearful" and "dismissive" sort. Consider the main two fearful and three dismissive arguments:

Fearful concern 1: CBDC would cause structural bank disintermediation , uncontrolled capital flows, the ballooning of the central bank balance sheet and an implied centralisation of credit allocation (through central bank choices on asset allocation and the collateral framework), and in the case of banking crises, the facilitation of bank runs (Cecchetti & Schoenholtz, 2021; Quarles, 2021; Waller, 2021). The authors however do not discuss or try to falsify the proposals to address these issues, such as in Kumhof and Noone (2018) and Bindseil and Panetta (2021). The latter argue that a system of tiered remuneration would be effective to control against bank disintermediation, with CBDC holdings beyond some threshold being discouraged by a sufficiently unattractive remuneration, which could be made even less attractive in the case of an exceptional banking crisis.

Fearful concern 2: CBDC would lead to an undue concentration of information on payments of citizens with the central bank, or generally an increase of power of central banks which is not in the interest of a civil democratic society. Generally central banks would be unable to find a good balance between preventing illicit payments and ensuring compliance on one side and protecting privacy. However, central banks generally indicate that they do not want to collect individual accountholder or payment data. On the contrary, central banks will aim to avoid through a correspondingly decentralised CBDC architecture. Moreover, data protection is a general matter of legislation and the preferences of society and can be legislated in a democracy, and obviously central banks will be keen to strictly apply all data protection requirements established by the legislator. Finally, national security authorities, who are interested in payments data, typically have access to private retail payment data from a technical perspective, and it is again a matter for the legislator and government to not allow their actual access or to define the conditions under which that access takes place. To this end, the introduction of CBDC does not change the fact that electronic payments are normally not anonymous and leave a data trail that might be accessed by security authorities and that preventing misuse is a matter of an effective government defining and monitoring the appropriateness of such data access.

Dismissive concern 1: Private solutions are highly efficient, serve well all relevant use cases and continue improving For example Cecchetti and Schoenholtz (2021) are right to point out the enormous progress in retail payments thanks to digitalisation and the improved services from which customers benefit. However, this is also the reason why the current form of central bank money available to all (i.e. banknotes), is at risk to become less and less attractive in relative terms and be marginalised over time, such that the current two-layer monetary architecture and the convertibility of commercial bank money into central bank money are significantly weakened. The enormous progress achieved on the side of private electronic payment instruments emphasises what progress central banks would refuse to apply to central bank money available to all if they would stick exclusively to banknotes.

Dismissive concern 2: Problems with private payment instruments can be addressed through regulation CBDC-critical authors have argued that problems arising with the reliance on private electronic payment instruments, such as e.g. financial stability, privacy, security, prevention of illicit payments, or abuse of-market-power can all be addressed through regulation, and that therefore CBDC is not needed nor adequate to cure any of those. It is true that regulation is crucial in the domain of retail payments, but this does not mean that regulation alone can preserve the advantages of a two-layer monetary system. Moreover, regulation is rarely fully effective, and in view of the importance of payments in modern society, complementing private payments by a public retail payments instrument still makes sense.

Dismissive concern 3: CBDC will struggle to be competitive because central banks lack expertise and comparative advantage in this field and also lack the flexibility and strong incentives prevailing in the private sector which are the basis for offering competitive products in a dynamic environment (e.g. Bofinger & Haas, 2021). However, CBDC has a number of powerful selling points and it seems more a matter of the central bank being willing to use them, such as unmatched safety, economies of scale, legal tender status, no abuse of eventual market power, etc. Also, central banks have demonstrated their ability to develop and run complex market infrastructures, including 24/7 instantaneous settlement infrastructures for retail payments.

9.4.3 Flow of Funds of CBDC Creation and Transfers

The creation of CBDC is captured in the financial account system in Table 9.3. If **households substitute banknotes with CBDC**, then the central bank and commercial bank balance sheets do not really change. However, if **households substitute commercial bank deposits with CBDC**, then this would imply a funding loss for commercial banks and could lead to "disintermediation" of the banking sector. In particular sight deposits with low remuneration could be expected to shift at least to some extent into riskless CBDC, leading to a loss of commercial banks' funding of equal size. Banks would have to try to offer better conditions on their deposits in

Table 9.3 Flow of funds into CBDC

Country X – in currency X			
Household 1			
Real goods	X	Equity	X
Other assets	X		
Deposits at bank	X -b		
CBDC	+a +b		
Banknotes	X -a		
Bank X			
Other assets	X	Deposits	X -b
Deposits at central bank	X -b +c	Credit central bank	X +c
		Equity	X
Central Bank X			
Credit to banks	X +c	Deposits of banks	X -b +c
Other assets	X	Banknotes issued	X -a
		CBDC	X +a +b
		Equity	X

order to protect their deposit base as much as possible – but this would imply higher funding costs for banks and a loss of commercial bank "seignorage".

Below, the creation of CBDC has thus been split into two parts: "a" where banknotes are substituted for CBDC; and "b" where deposits with banks have been substituted for CBDC. The effect of **flow a** on the rest of the financial accounts is neutral, but the effects of **flow b** are not: the substitution of deposits for CBDC lengthens the central bank balance sheet and central bank credit operations will have to fill the funding gaps of the banks, shown via the **flow c** (note that flow c may be different from flow b if for example flow b is compensated partially by a reduction of excess reserve holdings).

The substitution of deposits into CBDC (i.e. **flow b**) has an impact on funding costs of the banking system, as typically central bank credit is more expensive than the remuneration rate of sight deposits. Moreover, a larger recourse to central bank credit could make collateral scarcity more acute and thereby make the central bank collateral framework crucial from a credit allocation perspective, implying a centralisation of the credit provision process.

If flows of deposits into CBDC have an impact on average funding costs of banks, then also bank lending rates would have to increase, which in turn might require the central bank to lower its monetary policy interest rates to restore the appropriate financial conditions consistent with the monetary policy stance. In the new equilibrium, banks would have lost competitiveness and will lose some market share relative to other forms of funding (through capital markets and non-bank intermediaries).

Some have also promoted the idea of "synthetic CBDC", or "two-layer CBDC" , which is actually similar to a sort of stablecoin or e-money institution backed by central-bank money. Between the central bank and the ultimate holder of synthetic CBDC is a private CBDC intermediary, who is not only a distribution agent, but is also a full legal intermediary in the sense that they issue the monetary liabilities and have a claim on the central bank. In the instance where monetary liabilities are always 100% backed (in case of operational failures or fraud), there could be losses to the ultimate money holders stemming from an inability of the private entity to deliver on its convertibility promise. If such a construct is meant to be as close as possible to "synthetic CBDC", the central bank would need to (i) impose interoperability requirements to the monetary liabilities issued by the different issuers; (ii) be prescriptive on the way the intermediaries are designed, such as to ensure that their intermediation does not risk to undermine the soundness of their liabilities under any circumstances, relative to their underlying assets (central bank money); (iii) supervise the entities closely. Still, the central bank should make clear that the means of payments issued by these entities is not central bank money, and that the central bank does not accept liability for them.

In the examples presented below, we assume (without loss of generality) that Household 1 initially acquires CBDC in the value of "a" via the substitution of commercial bank deposits, and that Bank 1 compensates the outflow via central bank

Table 9.4 Single-layer CBDC

Country X – in currency X			
Household 1			
Real goods	X +b	Equity	X
Other assets	X		
Deposits at bank	X -a		
CBDC	+a -b		
Household 2			
Real goods	X -b	Equity	X
Other assets	X		
Deposits at bank	X		
CBDC	+b		
Bank			
Other assets	X	Deposits H1	X -a
Deposits at central bank	X	Deposits H2	X
		Credit central bank	X +a
		Equity	X
Central Bank			
Credit to banks	X +a	Deposits of banks	X
Other assets	X	Banknotes issued	X
		CBDC household 1	+a -b
		CBDC household 2	+b
		Equity	X

credit (**a**). Table 9.4 represents the case of a true one-layer CBDC, while Table 9.5 shows the case of "synthetic" i.e. two-layer CBDC, or a fully prefunded stablecoin or e-money. In both cases, a transfer of CDBC between the two households occurs following Household 1 purchasing a stock of real goods from Household 2 (**b**). In the case of synthetic CBDC, it is assumed that Household 1 has a CBDC account with s-CBDC issuer 1 (and likewise, Household 2 has a CBDC account with s-CBDC issuer 2). On the basis that sufficient interoperability exists between the issuers of synthetic CBDC, a stock of synthetic CBDC is therefore able to be transferred between the two households.

9.4.4 Issuing a CBDC: The Many Design Challenges in Practice

Beyond the basic architectural questions, designing a CBDC is a multidimensional undertaking involving various retail payment back-end and front-end layer issues. Consider the following overview of design issues:

Scope of a CBDC : the functionality and use cases of CBDC should depend on the gaps in the availability and practicality of central bank money, and/or where CBDC could plausibly offer better value and efficiency for society than private solutions. When designing a CBDC from scratch there is a temptation to give it comprehensive, state-of-the art functionality to base it on the most innovative technology and to cover as many use cases as possible. On this basis, it has been suggested that CBDC

Table 9.5 Synthetic (two-layer) CBDC

Country X – in currency X			
Household 1			
Real goods	X +b	Equity	X
Other assets	X		
Deposits at bank	X -a		
s-CBDC issuer 1	+a -b		
Household 2			
Real goods	X -b	Equity	X
Other assets	X		
Deposits at bank	X		
s-CBDC issuer 2	+b		
Bank X			
Other assets	X	Deposits H1	X -a
Deposits at central bank	X	Deposits H2	X
		Credit central bank	X +a
		Equity	X
s-CBDC issuer 1			
Account with central bank	+a -b	Stablecoin	+a -b
s-CBDC issuer 2			
Account with central bank	+b	Stablecoin	+b
Central Bank X			
Credit to banks	X +a	Deposits of banks	X
Other assets	X	Banknotes issued	X
		Account of s-CBDC 1	+a -b
		Account of s-CBDC 2	+b
		Equity	X

should: (i) be offered in various forms, including cards, mobile payments and desktop access, and be as convenient as existing private solutions; (ii) allow fully anonymous payments to protect privacy; (iii) allow offline payments; (iv) permit instant credit transfers to any commercial bank account and direct debits; (v) be programmable and allow "smart contracts" for advanced uses in industry and commerce; (vi) promote financial inclusion (i.e. be usable by those without bank accounts or mobile phones); (vii) be available for international use, so as to improve cross-border payments and strengthen the international role of the currency. Supporters of a broad functional scope for CBDC argue that a central bank is in a unique position in terms of credibility and economies of scale, such that even very significant investments in a comprehensive CBDC based on new technology can easily be justified, at least in large currency areas. Advocates also claim that an excessively narrow scope may make CBDC insufficiently attractive, leading to low demand, so the potential benefits remain unachieved. On the other hand, supporters of narrower functional scope may want to reduce risks of an excessive crowding out the private sector. They maintain that a broad-scope CBDC could prove to be a project that is very hard to manage, and that broad scope may go beyond user and policy needs, making it inefficient. The payments industry provides numerous examples of promising functionality and technologies which ultimately did not take off. This dichotomy between narrow and broad scope suggests there may be benefits to using open architecture, so additional functionalities can be added as they become sufficiently clear.

Business model (or "compensation" model) : every private payment instrument relies on a so-called business model, which determines who contributes to the costs through fees, and which player within the scheme gets which shares of these fees collected as a compensation. For example, card schemes like Visa or MasterCard set a merchant fee, and this merchant fee is shared between the card issuing bank, the acquiring bank, and the scheme provider (see e.g. Chap. 3). The business model for a CBDC needs to encourage the various players in the retail payments industry to actively promote its adoption and use. Three key stakeholders of a CBDC need to be taken into account in the design of the CBDC business model: consumers, merchants and supervised intermediaries. Payments are a two-sided market with network effects, so incentives also depend on actions taken by others and initially conflicting interests need to be reconciled through the design of financial compensation flows.

Integration and efficiency versus distinguishability and autonomy of a CBDC relative to the private sector payments ecosystem : the design of CBDC needs ideally to simultaneously achieve (1) a minimization of industry investment costs for the implementation of a CBDC (by relying on existing standards, etc.); (2) not producing undue dependence of the central bank from the industry; (3) not crowding out private initiatives (unless this is the intention); and (4) offering a distinct value proposition for citizens (distinguishability). Banknotes were well distinguishable and independent from private electronic money payment instruments. This is less the case in a digital world, when everybody would pay digitally and private electronic payments instruments co-exist with CBDC. The distinguishability of CBDC needs to be actively looked for and be designed in a way that ideally also makes sense economically (i.e. not only seek distinguishability for the sake of itself). Against this backdrop, numerous practical questions arise. For example, should a CBDC have its own mobile app, or should it be integrated into the payment mobile apps of banks and other payment services providers? A central bank may wish to facilitate the visibility and branding of its CBDC payment and liquidity management services through a separate mobile app available to citizens and merchants. It may also prefer the higher degree of control and independence that comes with a separate app, and the ability to control the privacy of payments data, for example. On the other hand, a separate CBDC mobile payment app needs to be designed and maintained and be served, perhaps by specialised providers who are independent from the dominant other payment services providers. Distinguishability could moreover be supported by having functionality and features that private sector solutions do not offer, such as offline payments, enhanced privacy or uncommon form factors (e.g. a smart card with display and biometric recognition). On each of such features, the central bank needs to understand why the private sector has not delivered on these features, as it can well be that customer demand was not really strong enough in practice, or that negative side effects were significant (e.g. offline and privacy might imply lower security and higher vulnerability against fraud, etc.). Ideally, the central bank could identify a convincing narrative why a feature that private instruments do not offer make sense in the context of CBDC.

Offline usage : currently, almost all private payment instruments are "online" i.e. a payment requires an internet connection which allows verification in central databases, including the availability of funds on the account that is to be debited. However, there have also been large-scale attempts to introduce off-line payment solutions, such as in particular pre-paid cards with hardware elements on which funds could be pre-loaded, such that at the moment of payment the debiting only needed to be recorded in the chip of the card. However, these attempts have not been too successful as usage was weak and did not support maintaining these systems despite large deployment costs. In the case of CBDC, it could be argued that one reason for central banks to prepare for CBDC issuance is the decline in the use of banknotes, which are obviously an offline instrument, and that therefore the demand for off-line electronic payments could increase together with the decline in banknotes use. The main challenge with off-line payments is security. The safest approach to control for security issues is to rely on secure hardware components and limit the size of payments that can be made offline.

Legal tender : Bossu et al. (2020, 66–70) discuss various legal aspects of CBDC including the question of legal tender status. They define as "legal tender status" the granting by law to a means of payment or currency "the power to validly and definitively extinguish monetary obligations ... By tendering a means of payment with legal tender status to the creditor, the debtor of a monetary obligation validly discharges his/her obligation." They also note that how this is legally achieved differs across jurisdictions in practice. For example, legal tender status may be waved contractually by parties to the transaction, and this may take the form of an announcement at the entrance in the shop that if a customer enters they waive the right to use cash granted by legal tender status and accept contractually to pay electronically. Regarding the digital euro, the European Commission (2022, section 1) explains:

> The concept of legal tender of euro cash...implies: (i) a general obligation in principle of acceptance of cash by the payee (ii) at full face value (iii) for the settlement of the monetary debt by a payer. Since a retail digital euro would be another form (digital, not physical) of central bank money, it could also be given legal tender status, as is the case for banknotes and coins. Legal tender status should ensure a wide acceptance of the digital euro.

Legal tender status, if effectively enforced and if the options to waive it contractually are constrained can strongly support the usage of CBDC. At the same time, it raises some questions in the context of a business model and a merchant fee, as the merchant would be both obliged to accept a CBDC and pay the related merchant fee.

"Programmable" money and payments : some have claimed that CBDC should cover highly innovative use cases, notably "programmability". Programmability can be understood in three ways:

- **Payments triggered by machines (which verify certain conditions) connected to the the payment network via application programming interfaces (APIs).** Even today, a 24/7 instant payment system could be accessed via APIs by any machine or computer code which verifies certain conditions to trigger a payment with immediate settlement. The scope and potential of such payments in commercial bank money has so far not been exhausted, although "open banking", being the access of commercial bank accounts via APIs by authorized third party providers, allows for it and has been enshrined in Europe in law through the PSD2 regulation (see Chap. 3). Payments can be called "programmable" as any program and conditionality can be set to trigger the payments.
- Some, like Deutsche Bundesbank (2020), **link the idea of programmable payments to the domain of blockchain and DLT**:

> Digital transformation is giving rise to new business models and is fundamentally changing existing business processes. .... Distributed ledger technology, which uses tokens to represent real goods and services and allows these to be traded digitally, makes it possible for flows of services to be programmable, autonomous and automated. This means that existing payment systems are set to be confronted with new challenges. The extent to which the advantages of digital settlement can be exploited is largely dependent on whether the associated cash flows will become equally programmable and can be synchronised with flows of services. Types of transactions that might conceivably require innovative solutions for cash leg settlement are largely based on DLT and might contain smart contracts that control their execution. Machine-to-machine payments, payments in the internet of things and pay-per-use payments are examples of use cases that require programmable payments to settle the cash leg.

- Critics of CBDC (e.g. the CATO institute), have expressed the fear that CBDC will be **programmable in the sense of allowing governments to impose constraints on the usage of money**, e.g. to not allow social welfare recipients to spend the money received on alcohol or cigarettes, or to prohibit everyone to purchase alcohol with CBDC after 10 p.m. Central banks investigating CBDC (e.g. the ECB) have denied that such features would even be considered.

Privacy : in a digitalized world in which more and more information flows take place online (shopping, chatting, dating, payments), and in which data storage is cheap and hackers have huge resources and often even government support (e.g. in Russia or North-Korea), there is a legitimate request by citizens to protect data. That the large majority of citizens, including many of those who claim to be fond of privacy, seem to care little in practice when being online, does not undermine the legitimacy of the right to claim privacy. In the case of the digital euro, data protection was highlighted as a key concern in several public consultations. The public may to a certain extent draw an analogy to cash as the current form of central bank money, which offers a high degree of privacy. At the same time, the processing of personal data may be necessary for specified purposes and is standard in electronic payments. For example, ensuring a necessary level of traceability of transactions (and therefore accepting the necessary information processing and temporary storage) is important to achieve (i) securely processed and provable payments; and (ii) compliance with rules against illicit activities, money laundering, terrorist financing and tax evasion. From a commercial perspective, payment data is particularly valuable for predicting future consumer interest and for allowing for targeted advertisement. Presumably any CBDC should allow users to opt out completely of a commercial usage of their personal CBDC payment data.

Technical solutions that best handle the above issues : whether retail CBDC should be based on "traditional" technology (like all current major private electronic payment solutions, like card schemes, mobile payment solutions, e-money, etc.) or whether it should rely on new technologies, such as DLT and blockchain, depends on the value added and risks that new technologies might bring. Centralized ledgers are familiar and well tested and allow for instant 24/7 settlement and programmability as well. In the case of the deployment of CBDC, and the somewhat lower agility and innovativeness of the public sector, and the need to preserve the reputation of the central bank, there may be a case for sticking with traditional technology first.

9.5 Conclusion: The Future of Money and Payments

As money and payments have been around for centuries and have attracted the attention of great minds since Aristoteles, Goethe's words "Who can think something stupid, who can think something smart, that the previous world didn't already think?"[1] apply. In numerous speeches and articles, policymakers and academics have invoked the current radical transformational power of digitalisation and new technology such as DLT and blockchain towards the nature of money and payments. But is the current period really outstanding? Could one not instead argue that the forms of money and payments have constantly evolved over the centuries across multiple dimensions, and that the basic issues of the nature and interaction between central bank and private means of payment have not changed? For example, Brunnermeier and Landau (2022, 19), amongst others, argue that it is "digitalisation" (in the particular sense of migration to DLT based technology) which allows almost anybody to create means of payment, and that this would be a reason for central banks to consider CBDC.

> In a digital world, (almost) anybody with some expertise in cryptography and computer science can create money. Not surprisingly, experiments in private money are now flourishing. The issuance of private money has been strongly reinvigorated by

[1] „Wer kann was Dummes, wer was Kluges denken, das nicht die Vorwelt schon gedacht?"Johann Wolfgang von Goethe, Faust. Der Tragödie zweiter Teil Faust II, Vers 6809 f. /Mephistopheles.

technology. . .Almost 9,000 cryptocurrencies are currently in use, some of them significant, many other marginal.

That everyone may try to create money however seems old and not linked to digitalisation or cryptography. For centuries, merchants or moneychangers could open a ledger and allow people to acquire deposits and make transfers to each other in book money. This succeeded at large scale in several flourishing late medieval city states in southern Europe, such as in Venice or Barcelona (see e.g. Kohn, 1999). It sometimes worked with the resulting private deposit banks achieving reputation and sizable giro payment volumes, but also created financial stability problems and interoperability issues, leading to regulation and the creation of early central banks, like the Taula de Canvi in Barcelona (at the beginning of the fifteenth century) and the Banco di Rialto of Venice (in the sixteenth century). In particular the latter was founded with extensive explicit reference to the financial stability concerns related to private money creation.

This being said, while the economics of money and payments are probably to a large extent "immutable" (to use a popular term of the Bitcoin community), changes in technology certainly matter, as some players may lose market share and are destabilised, and regulators and supervisors may fail to understand how the universal risks of money metamorphoses in the transition towards new forms can create regulatory ambiguity and financial instability. In the field of money and payments, the trend towards digitalisation has been and will continue to be transformational, making it unlikely that paper money will still be frequently used in a few decades. Some instruments and money issuers will benefit from this major transformation, while others will lose relevance. But unless central banks surprisingly stick forever with seventeenth century technology (i.e. banknotes) as far as their payment instruments issued to citizens are concerned, central bank money will continue to play a key role as means of payment.

References

Acemoglu, D. (2021). The Bitcoin Fountainhead, *Project Syndicate*, 5 Oct 2021, available at: https://www.project-syndicate.org/commentary/bitcoin-an-appealing-distraction-by-daron-acemoglu-2021-10

AMI-SeCo. (2021). The use of DLT in post-trade processes, report by the *Advisory Groups on Market Infrastructures for Securities and Collateral and for Payments*, April 2021, https://www.ecb.europa.eu/pub/pdf/other/ecb.20210412_useofdltposttradeprocesses~958e3af1c8.en.pdf?2779d0668b55434a0e67174b3f1183a4

Avoca. (2021). *Bitcoin: A trojan horse*, 14 Oct 2021, available at: https://www.linkedin.com/posts/activity-6854411140617818112-NpKx

Bank of International Settlements. (2022). *Annual report*. Bank of International Settlement.

Bindseil, U. (2019). *Central Banking before 1800: A rehabilitation*. Oxford University Press.

Bindseil, U., & Panetta, F. (2021). Central bank digital currency remuneration in a world with low or negative nominal interest rates. *VoxEU*. https://voxeu.org/article/cbdc-remuneration-world-low-ornegative-nominal-interest-rates

Bindseil, U., Papsdorf, P., & Schaaf, J. (2022). *The encrypted threat: Bitcoin's social cost and regulatory responses*, SUERF Policy Brief No. 262.

Bofinger, P., & Haas, T. (2021). Central bank digital currencies risk becoming a gigantic flop. *VoxEU*. https://voxeu.org/article/central-bank-digital-currenciesrisk-becoming-gigantic-flop

Bossu, W., Itatani, M., Margulis, C., Rossi, A., Weenink, H., & Yoshinaga, A. (2020). *Legal aspects of central bank digital currency: Central bank and monetary law considerations*. International Monetary Fund. IMF Working Paper WP/20/254.

Brooks, S., Jurisevic, A., Spain, M., & Warwick, K. (2018). *A decentralised payment network and stablecoin, v0.7*. Havven. Available at: https://cryptorating.eu/whitepapers/Havven/havven_whitepaper.pdf

Brown, G. R. (2018). *The Corda platform: An introduction*. Available at: https://corda.net/content/corda-platform-whitepaper.pdf

Brunnermeier, M., & Landau, J. (2022). *The digital euro: Policy implications and perspectives*. STUDY – requested by the ECON Committee, European Parliament.

Cecchetti, S. G., & Schoenholtz, K. L. (2021). Central bank digital currency: The battle for the soul of the financial system. *VoxEU*. https://voxeu.org/article/central-bank-digital-currency-battle-soul-financial-system

CPMI-IOSCO. (2021). *Review of margining practices*. Bank of International Settlements.

De Nederlandsche Bank. (2022). *Crypto-assets: Evolution and policy response*, Occasional Study Nr 06 2022.

del Castillo, M., & Paz, J. (2022). ASX Chairman Apologizes After Writing Off $165 Million Blockchain Project.*F orbes*. https://www.forbes.com/sites/michaeldelcastillo/2022/11/16/seminal-blockchain-project%2D%2Dgoes-down-the-drain-chairman-apologizes/?sh=534f9ece17d3

Deutsche Bundesbank. (2020). *Money in programmable applications - Cross-sector perspectives from the German economy*, Frankfurt am Main, 21 December 2020. Available at: https://www.bundesbank.de/resource/blob/855148/ebaab681009124d4331e8e327cfaf97c/mL/2020-12-21-programmierbare-zahlung-anlage-data.pdf

De Vries, A. (2021). Bitcoin boom: What rising prices mean for the network's energy consumption. J. *oule, 5*(3), 509–513.

Diem. (2022). Statement by Diem CEO Stuart Levey on the Sale of the Diem Group's Assets to Silvergate. https://www.diem.com/en-us/updates/stuart-leveystatement-diem-asset-sale/#:~:text=Despite%20giving%20us%20positive%20substantive,have%20done%20today%20to%20Silvergate.

ECB. (2022). *What is TARGET Instant Payment Settlement (TIPS)?*. Available at: https://www.ecb.europa.eu/paym/target/tips/html/index.en.html.

European Commission. (2022). *Consultation document – Targeted consultation on a digital euro, DG-FISMA*.

G7 Working Group on Stablecoins. (2019). *Investigating the impact of global stablecoins*, October 2019, jointly published by the G7, IMF and CPMI.

IOSCO. (2022). *IOSCO decentralized finance report, OR01/2022*, March 2022.

Kohn, M. (1999). *Early deposit banking. Working Paper 99–03*, Dartmouth College.

Kolbert, E. (2021). Why bitcoin is bad for the environment. *The New Yorker*, published 22 April 2021. Available at: https://www.newyorker.com/news/daily-comment/why-bitcoin-is-bad-for-the-environment

Kumhof, M., & Noone, C. (2018). Central bank digital currencies - design principles and balance sheet implications. *Bank of England Staff Working Paper, No. 725*.

Libra. (2019). *Libra Association white paper*, June 2019.

Libra. (2020). *Libra Association white paper V2.0*, April 2020.

MakerDAO. (2017). The Dai Stablecoin System. Whitepaper. https://blog.bitmex.com/wpcontent/uploads/2018/06/DAI.pdf

Malekan, O. (2022). *Re-architecting trust – The curse of history and the crypto cure for money, markets and platforms*. Triple Smoke Stack.

Nakamoto, S. (2008). *Bitcoin: A peer-to-peer electronic cash system*, Bitcoin Foundation, November 2008.

Panetta, F. (2020). *The two sides of the (stable)coin, Speech delivered at Salone dei Pagamenti*, 4 November 2020, published on ECB website.

Panetta, F. (2022). Crypto dominos: the bursting crypto bubbles and the destiny of digital finance. https://www.ecb.europa.eu/press/key/date/2022/html/ecb.sp221207_1~7dcbb0e1d0.en.html

Poon, J., & Dryja, T. (2016). *The Bitcoin lightning network: Scalable off-chain instant payments*, working paper.

Quarles, R. (2021). *Parachute Pants and Central Bank Money, Speech given on June 28, 2021 at the 113th Annual Utah Bankers Association Convention*. Sun Valley. https://www.federalreserve.gov/newsevents/speech/quarles20210628a.htm

Roberds, W., & Velde, F. R. (2014). *Early public banks*. Federal Reserve Bank of Atlanta Working Paper Series No. 1014–9.

Schar, F., & Berentsen, A. (2020). *Bitcoin, blockchain, and cryptoassets: A comprehensive introduction*. MIT press.

Seeman, B. (2022) *The Coinmen*. Independently Published.

Tether. (2016). Tether: Fiat currencies on the Bitcoin blockchain. tether.to.

Taleb, N., & N. (2021). Bitcoin, currencies, and fragility. *Quantitative Finance, 21*(8), 1249–1255.

Ugolini, S. (2017). *The evolution of central banking: theory and history*. Palgrave Macmillan.

Waller, C. (2021). CBDC: A Solution in Search of a Problem?, Speech given on August 05, 2021 at the American Enterprise Institute, Washington, D.C.. https://www.federalreserve.gov/newsevents/speech/waller20210805a.htm

Index

U. Bindseil, G. Pantelopoulos, *Introduction to Payments and Financial Market Infrastructures*, Springer Texts in Business and Economics,
https://doi.org/10.1007/978-3-031-39520-8

GPSR Compliance
The European Union's (EU) General Product Safety Regulation (GPSR) is a set of rules that requires consumer products to be safe and our obligations to ensure this.

If you have any concerns about our products, you can contact us on

ProductSafety@springernature.com

In case Publisher is established outside the EU, the EU authorized representative is:

Springer Nature Customer Service Center GmbH
Europaplatz 3
69115 Heidelberg, Germany

www.ingramcontent.com/pod-product-compliance
Lightning Source LLC
Chambersburg PA
CBHW071602280926
52228CB00003B/28
9783031395192